STUDIES IN ECONOMICS AND BUSINESS

Labour Markets

Geoff Hale

Series Editor
Susan Grant
West Oxfordshire College

Heinemann

Heinemann Educational Publishers
Halley Court, Jordan Hill, Oxford OX2 8EJ
Part of Harcourt Education

Heinemann is a registered trademark of
Harcourt Education Limited

Text © Geoff Hale, 2001

First published in 2001

05 04 03 02
10 9 8 7 6 5 4 3 2

British Library Cataloguing in Publication Data
A catalogue record for this book is available from the British Library

ISBN 0 435 33219 8

Typeset by TechType, Abingdon, Oxon
Printed in Great Britain by Biddles Ltd, *www.biddles.co.uk*

Acknowledgements
The publishers would like to thank the following for permission to reproduce
copyright material: Atlantic Syndication and *The Evening Standard,* p. 107;
AQA examination questions are reproduced by permission of the Assessment
and Qualification Alliance; *The Guardian,* pp. 29, 39 and 88 © *The
Guardian; The Independent,* pp. 19–20, 76 and 90; *The Northern Echo,* p.
117; *The Observer,* pp. 52, 60 and 72 © *The Observer,* p. 34 © Jim Pollard
p. 114 © Richard Reeves; OCR examination questions reproduced with the
kind permission of OCR; *The Sunday Times* for *The Sunday Times* Pay List
2000, p. 27, and *The Sunday Times* Rich List 2000, p. 86 © Times Newspapers
Limited 2000.

The publishers have made every effort to contact copyright holders. However,
if any material has been incorrectly acknowledged, the publishers would be
pleased to correct this at the earliest opportunity.

Tel: 01865 888058 www.heinemann.co.uk
ii

Contents

Preface		*iv*
Introduction		*1*
Chapter One	The markets for labour	*3*
Chapter Two	Wage determination	*22*
Chapter Three	Labour markets and market failure	*31*
Chapter Four	Government intervention	*43*
Chapter Five	Employment and unemployment	*56*
Chapter Six	The distribution of income and wealth	*78*
Chapter Seven	Poverty	*92*
Chapter Eight	After work	*103*
Chapter Nine	Future trends	*112*
Conclusion		*121*
Index		*123*

Preface

Recently the Government has done much to change the framework within which labour markets operate in the UK, directives from the European Union are having a greater impact, we are increasingly aware of the global nature of the economic system and even A-levels have changed. This book attempts to address these changes by raising the key issues and explaining points in a clear and accessible way.

The Chapters are intended to pick out the main headings used by the examination boards so that the information will be easily related to the various AS and A2 Economics Specifications. The book should also prove useful to students of Business Studies either at A-level, or VCE, anyone approaching Labour Markets for the first time on an undergraduate course or, indeed, the general reader looking for an insight into what makes labour markets tick.

The author, Geoff Hale, is a very experienced teacher and A-level and GCSE examiner who has been at the forefront of a number of curriculum developments in Economics. He has written widely on the subject and has had a significant number of articles and books published. He is currently co-ordinator of the Cornwall Union Learning Centre.

Introduction

'I work about 27 hours a day and have no time whatsoever to go shopping.'
Martha Lane Fox, founder of *lastminute.com*

Economics looks at the way in which people, organizations and countries make decisions about how their scarce resources will be used. Labour is one of those scarce resources. Governments rely in large part on the market system to determine how labour will be used, but how effective is the system?

Work is essential to our lives. Most of us grow up in households where at least one person, or increasingly two, goes out to work. Work and the payment we receive for it determines our lifestyle, provides us with the means to satisfy our wants and needs and even defines who we are. Work gives us enjoyment, a ready-made social group, a challenge for our talents, status and, often, our partners. If we lose our job it is a disaster. Redundancy is never an appealing idea. In Japan they commit suicide over the loss of face. The work ethic is still a strong driving force in society and, as an alternative to religion, provides an effective means of social control.

The way we engage with the world of work shapes our lives. For most of the time we do not feel part of any market system. It seems to happen around us and yet we are part of the labour market. Some, with particular talents, can manipulate the market to their advantage but most of us cannot.

The aim of this book is to lead readers through the complexities of the subject towards achieving a comprehensive understanding. It looks at the ways in which labour markets work, the problems and issues affecting these markets, the influence groups try to exert on them, the changes affecting labour markets and what happens after we have left the markets.

Chapter One clarifies what a labour market is and that there are many different but related active labour markets in the UK. How do labour markets differ from product markets?

Chapter Two looks at what determines wage levels, the part that the forces of supply and demand play in fixing wages, the effects of elasticity and the changing patterns of demand for labour. Do people receive their just desserts in the labour markets?

Chapter Three explains why labour markets fail, the impact trade unions have on the market and the effects of discrimination in the labour market. Is equal pay between men and women achievable?

Chapter Four examines the role the government plays in attempting to correct labour market failure including the National Minimum Wage and employment legislation. Is the government always correct in its judgment?

Chapter Five considers issues associated with employment and unemployment covering the definition, causes, costs and solutions to unemployment. Is there a 'natural' or equilibrium rate of unemployment?

Chapter Six reviews the factors influencing the distribution of income and wealth and explains the various ways in which income and wealth might be redistributed. To what extent should income be redistributed?

Chapter Seven focuses on the issue of poverty both in the UK and in the developing countries. How can poverty be reduced?

Chapter Eight discusses the effects of the UK's ageing population and the implications this will have on working arrangements and pensions. How will the economy need to adapt to the growing numbers of older people?

Chapter Nine surveys the range of issues which have been seen to affect labour markets in the UK and considers how these might project into the future. Will labour markets be subject to greater government intervention?

Enjoy!

Chapter One

The markets for labour

'Haynes is an entertainer, if the maximum wage is ever abolished, I will pay him what he is worth, which is £100 a week.'
Tommy Trinder, Chairman of Fulham Football Club, 1961. The nation gasped. At the time Johnny Haynes was the England football captain and widely regarded as the best footballer in the country.

Markets are magical or at least seem to possess magical qualities. If left to themselves, markets solve the big economic questions about what to produce, how to produce and who should receive the goods and services once they have been produced. The free market system happily chugs away without interference making these key decisions with the supporters of free markets able to claim that it is the most cost efficient and neutral way to allocate the world's scarce resources. Free markets have become closely linked to democracy and have been a major contributor to the defeat of communist, planned economies as their people seek a better quality of life.

At the beginning of the twenty-first century, the stock of free market economies has rarely been higher. We are all free marketeers now with the USA in the vanguard. But how do markets work and can the arguments that support free product markets also be applied to labour markets?

In practice, markets seem beautifully simple. People as consumers want to benefit from a wide range of goods and services. To earn the money to be able to buy these, they work for employers or themselves producing the products that others wish to buy. Successful businesses will respond to the demand from consumers making more of the most demanded and most profitable goods. Consumers will only be able to benefit from those goods they can afford to buy. Bargains will be struck at prices the consumer is prepared to pay and at which the business is content with the profit margin. Price will indicate the point at which the supply of the product meets the demand for the product and the market will be in equilibrium.

Generally, other things remaining the same, the lower the price the more will be demanded and the higher the price the more will be supplied. This produces the well-known scissor effect and is often shown by using a supply and demand diagram. If we take the example of the market for coffee we can see that as the price of coffee falls, more

3

will be bought as consumers buy coffee instead of other possible substitutes such as tea and also, as coffee gets cheaper, people will be able to afford to buy more coffee – their real income has increased. The demand curve for coffee slopes down from the top left of the graph to the bottom right.

The supply curve for coffee slopes in the opposite direction. At low prices few farmers will be prepared to produce coffee, other products will be far more profitable. But as the price rises, farmers see the prospect for making more profits by producing coffee and so more will be supplied possibly being taken from stocks held. The gradient of the demand and supply curves reflects the degree to which the demand or supply responds to changes in price although the exact slope will be dependent on the scales selected on each axis. If there is little response the curves will be steeper and the demand or supply will be relatively inelastic. If they change proportionately more when the price moves then the curves will be shallower and the demand or supply will be relatively elastic.

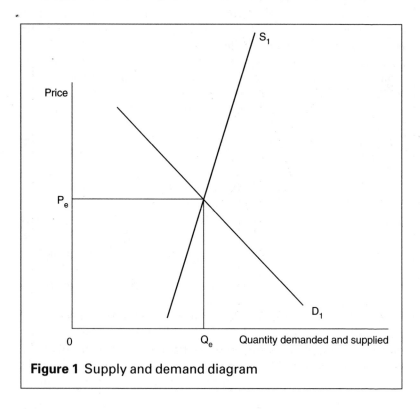

Figure 1 Supply and demand diagram

In Figure 1, S1 is the supply curve for coffee and supply is relatively inelastic reflecting the difficulty of increasing the supply of coffee in response to short term price changes. D1 is the demand curve for coffee. Equilibrium price is established where the forces of demand and supply meet at a price of Pe where the quantity of Qe is sold in the market.

This kind of analysis is conducted on the basis of a number of key assumptions. Firstly, price is the only factor in the market changing. If anything other than price changes such as a change in taste away from coffee on health grounds or poor coffee growing conditions causing crop yields to fall then the demand or supply curves will shift their position causing a new equilibrium price to be established.

Figure 2 indicates that a change, such as bad growing conditions, has reduced supply and shifted the supply curve from S1 to S2 causing the equilibrium price to rise to P1 and the quantity of coffee traded in the market to fall to Q1. If more people now decide to drink coffee then the

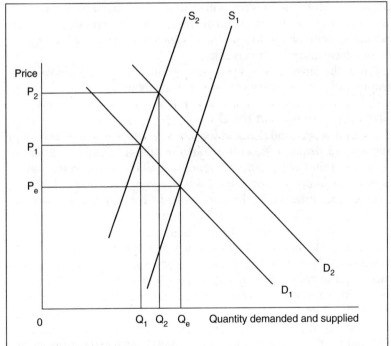

Figure 2 Diagram showing shifts in the demand and supply curves and new equilibrium prices

demand curve shifts to D2. Competition between buyers forces price up to P2 with Q2 being bought and sold.

The beauty of the analysis is that the quantities supplied and demanded in the market are automatically brought into line at the new equilibrium price.

In practice, the system is far murkier but the question is whether it is helpful to apply such a model to the labour market. To answer this we need to investigate the particular characteristics of the labour market to see how it might be different to a product market such as coffee.

It is clear that there are many different labour markets. The labour markets in Scotland, Swansea or Swindon will differ greatly – there will be regional or local labour markets which are broadly separate from each other. The market for computer engineers will be different to the market for sales staff – there will be labour markets for different skills and there will be labour markets for different jobs such as the employees of supermarkets and call centres. Men and women may face different labour markets as will people from different ethnic groups. Markets for full-time workers will be different to markets for part-time workers. The way we engage with labour markets will depend on us acting as individuals for we have our own agenda with regards employment and what it may offer.

Given the range of labour markets on offer we shall begin with the features and characteristics of the national labour market.

The labour market in the UK

There is a supply and demand for labour in the UK just as there is a supply and demand for coffee. But the labour market is different. Analysis of the coffee market assumes that all the coffee on the market is the same in every respect: it is homogeneous. Each unit of labour is likely to be different to the next with different skills, abilities and motivation. Coffee can be moved around to search out the highest price, labour is less mobile. Family connections or friends often keep people in particular parts of the country even if much better wages are being paid elsewhere. The price of houses may form a barrier to the movement of people but will not hinder the movement of coffee beans. People demand coffee beans to make and enjoy coffee, employers demand workers not for their own sake but to produce goods or services. The demand for labour is a **derived demand** gained from the demand for the products produced. Greater demand for coffee means greater demand for people to produce coffee. Coffee prices may rise and fall in response to market conditions, wages tend to be **sticky**: they may rise but falls will be resisted. Some workers form trade unions to help the resistance. The union for coffee beans has yet to make much of an impact.

The supply of labour

In 1999 there were 46.2 million people over the age of 16 of which 28.9 million were economically active forming the working population. Of these, 27.2 million were in employment and 1.7 million were unemployed so the total supply of labour is approaching 29 million people. The number is important since the larger the number of economically active people the greater the number of people is contributing to the creation of wealth for the nation.

Factors affecting the supply of labour

As the total size of the population increases so it is likely that the size of the working population will rise. However, much depends on what is causing the population to increase. Populations can rise due to natural increase through an increase in the **birth rate** or reduction in the **death rate**. These measure the number of live births or number of deaths per thousand of the population. In the last century, 1920 recorded the highest number of births at 1.13 million and a figure greater than one million has only been recorded in two years since: 1947 and 1964. Since 1973 the number of births has remained relatively steady at about 700,000 and it is not expected to change significantly but may drift down a little. A lower birth rate could increase the size of the workforce as fewer women take time out from work to have their children. There is a trend to have fewer children per family and women are choosing to plan their career, delay pregnancy until later on and then return to work to maintain their financial independence. The more widespread availability and lower cost of childcare arrangements may also make the return to work easier.

The death rate has also been falling with improvements in medical knowledge, diet and living conditions but as this happens there will be a growing number of people dependent on the workforce to create the wealth of the nation. Just over 620,000 people died in 2000 (almost the same number as had died in 1900 but with a much smaller population). Births exceeded deaths by 90,000 in 2000 and this gives the natural growth rate of the population.

Population can also be increased by **net migration**: the balance of immigration set against emigration. There has been a net gain through migration since the 1980s and the number has risen in recent years due to international unrest and civil wars driving people out of their own country. The greater number of asylum seekers has pushed the immigrant numbers to above 150,000 in 2000 but as international disputes are settled, the numbers should fall back to about 95,000 per year. Some of the more extreme political groups try to make some capital of this but immigrants do bring real benefits. They are mostly young, prepared to work hard (often at low pay) to make a successful life for themselves and take on jobs which might, otherwise, have not been filled. They add skills and numbers to the UK workforce.

Encouraging immigration can be a very effective way of boosting the supply of particular types of worker. In the past the UK has exploited its colonial connections to attract people to fill job vacancies and there has been a similar strategy recently to recruit people for jobs in education, the health service and social care.

The supply of labour is affected by the number of people in different age groups or the age structure of the population. The higher the percentage of people below school leaving age or above retirement age the lower the workforce will be. After the Second World War there was an increase in the birth rate – the post war baby boom. This group is now into its 50s and will soon be leaving the workforce causing a reduction in its size.

This point is also linked to the school-leaving and retiring ages. Although the actual school-leaving age has remained at 16, an increasing number of young people are staying on in education and going on to higher education cutting down the numbers entering the workforce. At the other end of the scale, some people have been looking to retire earlier or have been forced into that situation by the cost cutting decisions of employers. By 2010 there will be harmonization of the retiring ages between men and women with women's retirement age rising to 65. This will lead to more women remaining in the workforce. As people's health improves and they live longer many people may wish to extend their working lives by carrying on working into their 70s.

The gender balance of the population will affect the numbers of people at work. There tend to be more women than men in the population. Women live longer than men and tend to suffer less from the major killer diseases of cancer and heart disease. A higher proportion of men than women are in employment due to the career breaks women take when raising families and so if there are a larger number of men in the population there will be a larger workforce. However, this is changing to some extent and it is the case that a much higher proportion of women are now choosing to develop careers of

Table 1 Growth of population and net migration

	Annual averages (thousands)					
	Population at start of period	Live births	Deaths	Net natural change	Net migration and other	Overall change
Census enumerated						
1901–1911	38,237	1,091	624	467	−82	385
1911–1921	42,082	975	689	286	−92	194
1921–1931	44,027	824	555	268	−67	201
1931–1951	46,038	785	598	188	25	213
Mid-year estimates						
1951–1961	50,287	839	593	246	6	252
1961–1971	52,807	963	639	324	−12	312
1971–1981	55,928	736	666	69	−27	42
1981–1991	56,352	757	655	103	43	146
1991–1998	57,808	748	637	112	93	204
Mid-year projections						
1998–2001	59,237	714	630	84	155	239
2001–2011	59,954	701	614	87	95	182
2011–2021	61,773	712	620	92	95	187

	Inflow			Outflow			Balance		
	Persons	Males	Females	Persons	Males	Females	Persons	Males	Females
1988	216	109	107	237	125	113	−21	−15	−6
1989	250	110	140	205	108	97	44	1	43
1990	267	135	132	231	113	118	36	22	14
1991	267	122	144	239	120	119	28	2	26
1992	216	99	117	227	113	114	−11	−14	3
1993	213	101	112	216	113	103	−2	−12	10
1994	253	126	127	191	92	98	62	34	28
1995	245	130	115	192	102	90	54	28	26
1996	272	130	143	216	105	111	56	24	32
1997	285	143	142	225	121	103	60	22	38
1998	332	167	165	199	100	99	133	68	66

their own and stay in employment if at all possible. Over the years the balance between male and female workers has changed. The decline in some sections of industry, particularly traditional employment such as

Table 2 Economically active men and women

LABOUR MARKET SUMMARY Labour Force Survey summary: all, seasonally adjusted (000s)

UNITED KINGDOM SEASONALLY ADJUSTED	All	Total Economically Active	Total in employment	ILO unemployed	Economically Inactive	Economic activity rate (%)	Employment rate (%)	ILO unemployment rate (%)	Economic Inactivity rate (%)
All people Aged 16–59(W)/64(M) Spring quarters (Mar–May)									
1988	34,772	27,762	25,284	2,477	7,010	79.8	72.7	8.9	20.2
1989	34,908	28,061	26,007	2,054	6,847	80.4	74.5	7.3	19.6
1990	35,018	28,216	26,246	1,970	6,802	80.6	75.0	7.0	19.4
1991	35,103	28,118	25,713	2,404	6,986	80.1	73.3	8.6	19.9
1992	35,174	27,855	25,056	2,799	7,318	79.2	71.2	10.0	20.8
1993	35,242	27,762	24,799	2,963	7,481	78.8	70.4	10.7	21.2
1994	35,337	27,773	25,002	2,771	7,564	78.6	70.8	10.0	21.4
1995	35,483	27,807	25,308	2,499	7,676	78.4	71.3	9.0	21.6
1996	35,663	28,018	25,645	2,373	7,645	78.6	71.9	8.5	21.4
1997	35,844	28,182	26,118	2,063	7,663	78.6	72.9	7.3	21.4
1998	36,026	28,263	26,460	1,803	7,763	78.5	73.4	6.4	21.5
1999	36,177	28,532	26,754	1,778	7,645	78.9	74.0	6.2	21.1

Source: *Labour Force Surveys, January 2001*

coal, steel, shipbuilding and textiles has hit mainly male employment. Long periods of unemployment have led to some men becoming discouraged and they have consequently dropped out of the workforce or have taken early retirement due to illness. Increasing divorce rates have created more lone parent families. Women have seen the need to establish a greater degree of financial independence and this has encouraged many back into the more flexible working hours of the service sector.

It is possible to construct a supply curve for labour with the numbers of people willing to offer their services for work increasing as the wage levels rise. The price offered for labour will affect the supply.

At wage level W1 wage rates are low and fewer people will be prepared to give up their time to work and may prefer to survive on state benefits. As wages rise to W2 it now becomes more worthwhile for people to work, as they can be much better off in work than on benefit and the quantity supplied increases to Q2. Certainly the introduction of the **National Minimum Wage** in 1998 which raised the lowest rates of pay appears to have had this effect. The move to get

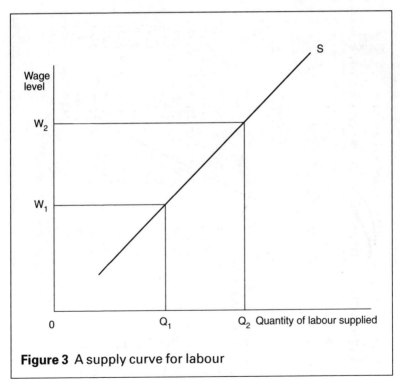

Figure 3 A supply curve for labour

more people back into work is improved if the tax rates on low pay are reduced so that people keep more of what they earn and the differential between income in work and income on benefit is increased. The government has given great attention to its efforts to reduce the **poverty trap** which stops people climbing their way out of poverty. As people achieve a wage rise then they lose access to certain benefits and may have to pay tax on the extra income earned. This could prevent some from taking employment. Tax cuts have helped and the rules for claiming benefits have been tightened to encourage further work participation, particularly of the young age groups.

Businesses recognize the link between higher pay and longer hours by their acceptance of the need to pay overtime rates if people work beyond their normal hours. However, there are limits to this. The price or wage paid for labour is not necessarily the only reason or the most important reason to supply labour. People see their wage as the route to a desired standard of living. At low wages many will choose to work long hours of overtime or do more than one job to boost their wage to the desired level. But as incomes rise people may prefer to have more

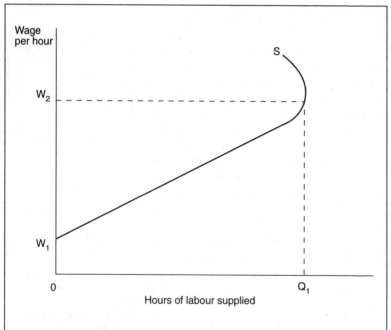

Figure 4 An individual's backward sloping supply curve of labour

leisure time: more time on the golf course instead of more time in the office. Figure 4 shows that the individual's supply curve of labour becomes backward sloping as they substitute leisure for work time.

If the wage offered is below W1 then the individual is not prepared to supply any time for work. As wages rise above W1 supply increases and continues to increase. But if wage rises above W2 then the individual would prefer to have more hours of leisure instead of work. One of the interesting implications of this is that increasing the wage either through wage rises or tax cuts may produce more hours work up to a point. But tax cuts for the high paid may lead to less time spent at work and more time spent on the golf course.

The generation that grew up in the 1960s and 70s experienced a world where going straight into work from school or college was the norm. Indeed, there was a choice of jobs awaiting the school leaver. Unemployment was not an option. In the 80s the situation changed. Attitudes towards work appeared to have changed, caused by a changing employment culture. Mass unemployment emerged and it became part of government policy to keep wages and the trade unions under control. A new generation of young people grew up where employment prospects were far less certain. In some parts of the country unemployment became the way of life. Some economists supported the notion that there was a **natural rate of unemployment** dependent on the institutional rigidity built into the labour market and if governments tried to get unemployment below this level the result would simply be more inflation. The Labour government, which came into office in 1997, took the view that this disaffected group would need both the carrot and stick treatment to get them back into the swing of work. If people do not possess the kinds of skills required by the employers of today then they could be considered as making themselves **voluntarily unemployed** and become excluded from the labour market. The policy to reduce this social exclusion has been essential as part of the general strategy to improve the life chances of this group and to redistribute income.

The labour supply must mean more than just the number of bodies offered to employers. It also depends on the number of hours people are prepared to spend at work. The decision to work involves an **opportunity cost** in that individuals forego their own leisure time to work for somebody else. People will be prepared to give up time if they believe that the benefits they receive, both monetary and non-monetary, outweigh the benefits they might have gained had they used that time in an alternative way. Table 3 shows that in the UK people tend to work long hours, in fact the longest in the European Union.

Table 3 Average hours worked in EU countries

Average hours usually worked[1] per week by full-time employees: by gender, EU comparison, 1998

	Hours	
	Males	*Females*
United Kingdom	45.7	40.7
Portugal	42.1	39.6
Greece	41.7	39.3
Spain	41.2	39.6
Germany	40.4	39.3
Luxembourg	40.3	37.4
France	40.3	38.7
Austria	40.2	39.8
Sweden	40.2	40.0
Finland	40.1	38.2
Italy	39.7	36.3
Denmark	39.3	37.7
Netherlands	39.2	38.5
Belgium	39.1	37.5
EU average[2]	41.3	39.0

[1] Excludes meal breaks but includes regularly worked paid and unpaid overtime.
[2] Average calculated with 1997 data for Irish Republic.
Source: *Labour Force Surveys,* Eurostat.

The **EU Working Time Directive**, which sets down a maximum working week of 48 hours, was introduced in 1998 but has yet to make a major impact in the UK. Employers are still able to skirt round the law by asking for 'volunteers' to work longer hours. Although this can be acceptable, it is often difficult for workers to opt out of such arrangements whilst retaining the goodwill and support of the employer. Also it is the case that many workers choose to spend far longer on their work than they are expected to by their employer. Many people not only enjoy their work but also get great satisfaction from it. In management this can lead to a culture of **presenteeism** where employees feel that they can impress by their dedication and commitment to work. Some City employers have even installed beds at the workplace. The **restructuring** and **de-layering** that firms have introduced and the search for efficiency have increased the work pressures on some and, consequently, stress levels in business have risen.

Do longer hours lead to greater economic efficiency and higher productivity? There is a debate about the answer to this question. Longer hours will result in a rise in total output but the efficiency of individual employees will decline with the extra hours worked. One response has been to promote the merits of **family friendly** working practices to achieve a better work/life balance. Some research suggests that this leads to more efficient working as well as a more satisfactory domestic life, in other words: better for the overall welfare of society.

The quality of the labour will be reflected in the productivity performance of the economy. Generally, we would expect that higher skill levels, education standards and qualifications of employees would accompany increased productivity and efficiency leading to higher living standards. The skill levels and attitudes to training and learning are particularly important when the changing nature of business is taken into account as we move towards a knowledge-based economy. So, how does the UK's workforce compare?

The Moser report *Improving Literacy and Numeracy: A Fresh Start* in 1999 revealed that approximately 7 million adults have difficulties in literacy and numeracy. One in five adults, when given the alphabetical index to the Yellow Pages, could not find the page for plumbers and people with poor basic skills are six times more likely to be out of work as those with good skills. In the mid 1990s 40% of people had NVQ level 2 qualifications or the equivalent in the UK compared with 60% in France and 65% in Germany. More British young people leave school at 16 compared to France and Germany and fewer stay on to higher education. However, the situation is improving. The government has set challenging targets to raise standards, the basic skills issue is being addressed and the numbers going on to university have never been higher. This should help to close the productivity gap of about 20% between the UK and its main competitors.

The other element essential to high productivity is the level of investment in new equipment. Highly qualified and able workers will still not perform well if they have to work with poor, out-of-date machinery. This has been a problem with British firms where the investment levels have been below those of our competitors. At the end of the 1990s the USA was investing about 3% of its total income on information technology. In the UK it was half this figure. There are a variety of possible explanations for this. It could be due to low profits of British business, the lack of long-term economic stability or the culture of short-termism which puts the demands of shareholders above the long-term growth of the business. Whatever the cause, low investment leads to low productivity.

The demand for labour

The demand for labour is a derived demand. At a national level, as the economy expands so firms will want to employ more people to produce more goods and services. During these growth or boom periods, unemployment falls. Economies tend not to move in straight lines. After the boom, economies often move into recession as the business cycle turns down. During this phase unemployment rises as firms lay off workers in an attempt to cut costs and stay in business. The demand for labour falls. Today, with the growing interdependence of economies, one country will be affected by the cycles of other countries and may be dragged into recession despite its best efforts. Over half the UK's trade is with the rest of the EU. If recession hits the EU, it will hit the UK. The demand for labour in the UK is affected by what may be happening in France, Germany or the USA.

The price or wage paid for labour will affect demand. Generally, the higher the wage which has to be paid to labour the less will be the demand but this has to be linked to the output or productivity of the labour. City lawyers may command huge salaries but they may contribute greatly to the profits of the company employing them. The contribution or output of a receptionist employed at the same company may be valued at a much lower level and so the pay will be far less.

The cost and efficiency of other factors of production will affect the demand for labour. Firms aim at efficient production and so try to employ the optimum mix of factors. New technology may well be cheaper and more reliable than humans so, as the cost of new equipment falls, machinery may be substituted for people and the demand for labour falls. However, technological progress has not seen a continuous and unstoppable decline in the demand for labour. New technology opens up gaps for new products which had never been foreseen. The demand for labour will shift into the production of these items. The development of the Internet illustrates this trend with the mushrooming of a whole range of services we never realized we needed. How many people owned a mobile telephone or a DVD player ten years ago?

Nationally, the interaction between the demand and supply of labour will determine the general level of wages although this is of limited benefit since there is, effectively, no national labour market. It does allow us to make broad comparisons between countries where we

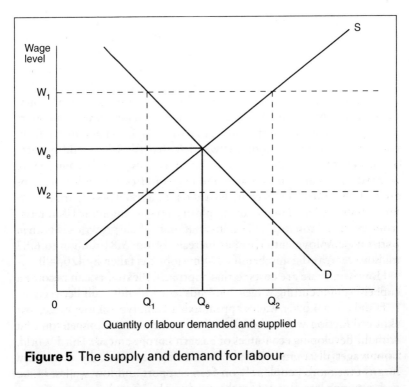

Figure 5 The supply and demand for labour

can see that, if wage levels differ, different supply and demand conditions prevail. The fact that countries in Eastern Europe and the Far East have much lower labour costs than the UK has forced UK businesses to look for production in goods and services where they can compete using other strengths.

In Figure 5 the equilibrium wage moves towards We and the analysis leads us to believe that if wages are held above the equilibrium level then the result will be unemployment. At a wage level of W1 the demand for labour is Q1 and the supply of labour Q2 so supply is greater than demand and so Q1 Q2 people are unemployed. If wages are below the equilibrium at, say W2, there will be full or over full employment and the result will probably be inflation, as employers need to push up wages just to hang on to their workers. The issues of employment and unemployment will be considered in more detail in Chapter 5.

The flexible labour market
Creating a flexible labour market was a main objective of UK governments during the 1980s and 90s. Taking the USA as a model, a

wide range of politicians believed, with some justification, that removing the obstacles to achieving a free labour market would create the conditions in which businesses and jobs could grow. Over the period 1990–98 the number of jobs created in the USA increased by 10.7% compared to 0.4% in the UK. Businesses generally welcome less controls on what they do and less red tape. Naturally, they would prefer to be able to impose their own wage rates, conditions and hours of work and hiring and firing policies without intervention from outside. Given this freedom, it was felt that the UK would become attractive to inward investors, businesses would become more profitable, expansion of the economy would occur and more jobs created. Prosperity and welfare would rise as a result. Comparing 1999 with 1989 the total number of people in employment in the UK did rise from 26.68 million to 27.25 million but most of the growth has been in part-time employment. This has increased from 5.81 million to 6.82 million whereas the number of full-time jobs has fallen by 420,000.

However, there are costs to this approach. Flexibility can become a euphemism for cutting wages that leads to a widening gulf between the rich and poor. Lower wages appeal to a certain type of low wage, low skill production where the UK will never be able to compete on cost with the developing economies of Eastern Europe and the Third World. Low wages discourage people from being economically active and means that more people rely on State support and low wages, in the end, meaning less demand for the goods and services firms are trying to sell.

KEY WORDS

Derived demand	Voluntary unemployment
Sticky wages	Opportunity cost
Birth rate	EU Working Time Directive
Death Rate	Presenteeism
Net migration	Restructuring
National Minimum Wage	De-layering
Poverty trap	Family friendly policies
Natural rate of unemployment	

Further reading
Anderton, A., Units 71 and 72 in *Economics*, 3rd edn, Causeway Press, 2000.

Davies, B., Hale, G., Smith, C., and Tiller, H., Chapter 2.9 in *Investigating Economics*, Macmillan, 1996.

Grant, S., and Vidler, C., Part 2 Unit 5 in *Economics in Context*, Heinemann, 2000.

Grant, S., Chapter 17 in Stanlake's *Introductory Economics*, 7th edn, Longman, 2000.

Annual Abstract of Statistics 2001

Social Trends 2001

Essay topics

1. (a) Discuss the factors which affect the supply of labour. [10 marks]
   (b) Assess how individuals may react to a change in the wage rate. [10 marks]

2. (a) Why is the demand for some groups of workers greater than that for others? [8 marks]
   (b) Discuss the extent to which demand alone is sufficient to explain differences in wage rates. [12 marks]

Source: OCR, Q2, Paper 4387, June 1996.

Data response question

Edexcel, Q2, Unit 5A, Specimen Paper, 2000.

Women in the workforce

The rise of women in the UK labour force

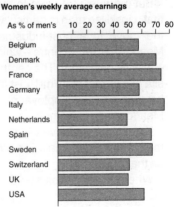

Women's weekly average earnings

Women are winning the piece on the jobs front. Fifty years ago, it was a man's world in the workplace. This year or next, there are likely to be more women employed than men, a prospect that has raised fears about the redundant rogue male. But is this apparent victory in the economic war of the sexes proving a real one?

In 1945, within a matter of months, two million women left the workforce. Britain was back to a world of jobs dominated by men. For every woman at work, there were two men, a ratio that remained largely unchanged for another 20 years. The post-war objective of full employment was seen as full-time jobs for men.

But in the past 15 years there has been another massive demobilization from the workforce. Except, this time, the economic drop-outs are more than a million men. Combine this with an increase of a million in the number of men who are still looking for jobs but cannot find them and the result is one of the highest rates of male non-employment in the western world.

Meanwhile, starting in the mid-1960s and gathering momentum in the last 15 years, women have grabbed more and more of the jobs. Result: there are now only a quarter of a million more male than female employees. When Mrs Thatcher became the first woman prime minister, the gap stood at 4 million. With pay rates still well behind those of men – weekly take-home earnings for full-time women are 70 per cent of male earnings – women have certainly formed a reserve army offering cheap labour for employers.

But there is a lot more to the female takeover of the workplace than that. Unskilled men in particular have found themselves wrong-footed by the move to a post-industrial economy. The staffing of Sheffield's Meadowhall retail centre – which has over half a million shoppers a week – tells its own story. The centre, which opened in 1990, was built on the site of a former steel mill, just the sort of heavy industry that once used to be such a heavy employer of men. But 78 per cent of the employees at Meadowhall are women.

Britain has a relatively high proportion of women in the workforce, but the US and Scandinavian countries such as Sweden score even higher on that count.

Where Britain does stand out is in combining this extent of female participation in work with a particularly low percentage of those whose jobs are full-time.

(Source: P Wallace, 'Women win a pyrrhic victory at work', *Independent on Sunday*, 7 May 1995)

(a) Identify the economic causes of the changing number of Trade Union members in the UK. [10 marks]

(b) How might the increase in female employment and the decrease in male employment be explained? [20 marks]

(c) Critically examine the factors which might explain the differences in women's and men's average earnings. [20 marks]

(d) Evaluate how EU labour market policies might affect wage differentials between men and women in the UK. [10 marks]

Total marks for Question: 60 marks

Chapter Two

Wage determination

'The cash didn't tempt me. I took the part because of the plot.'
Harrison Ford having just signed a contract to be paid $20m for 20
days' work on his film *The Widowmaker*.

The free market model

Why do some groups of workers earn more than others? If the labour
markets were totally free or 'perfect' markets, then the answer to this
question would be easy: there would be no differences, we would all
earn the same wage rate in the long run. A wage is a price and so
provides a signalling and rationing function to the market. If there were
a shortage of a particular type of labour, employers would be forced to
increase wages to attract workers to them and to ration out the existing
supplies of that kind of worker. The rise in wages of that group relative
to other groups would act as a signal and encourage other workers to
move into that area of work to take advantage of the higher wages; the
supply of labour would increase. As the supply increases so the wage
level falls and equilibrium is again reached but with a greater demand
and supply of that type of labour. All groups of labour would end up
earning the same wage rates, a curious outcome since this would be
similar to what we might expect from a totally planned economy.

The assumptions implicit in the free market model are rarely
achieved. Workers' **mobility** is severely restricted **industrially,
occupationally** and **geographically**. They tend not to want to change
jobs at the drop of a hat. People have their particular motivation and
often do not have the ability, skills or experience to change jobs very
easily. They cannot always move over long distances to take up jobs
and find it more difficult to move between countries. They simply may
not have the information about job vacancies available in other areas.
Job choice is based on many factors other than the wage level and even
employers would not welcome the continuous hiring and firing and
adjustments to wages required by the model.

Despite its limitations the free market model is a useful place to begin
our analysis. Employers demand labour because there is a demand for
the goods and services that the labour will produce. The demand is a
derived demand but employers appreciate that as more people are
employed the output gained from each extra worker will decline. If we

assume that a supermarket builds a new store and then considers how many people to employ, the first few will have great value since the shop can open and trade can begin. Shelves can be kept stocked and checkouts operated. Once all the checkouts are in operation extra people can have a value packing customers' bags but their contribution will be less than the first people employed. As more people are employed their value will continue to fall; the value of their marginal productivity will decline. This is represented in Figure 6.

The curve represents the employer's demand curve for labour. The first workers have a high value and are worth a lot to the employer; without them the store could not open. Successive workers have less value and, if the supermarket continued to take on workers, when point N2 is reached an extra employee has zero value and beyond that, employees get in the way and lead to a negative marginal value. In a perfect market this supermarket would be one of many employers taking on this kind of worker and the wage rate would be determined

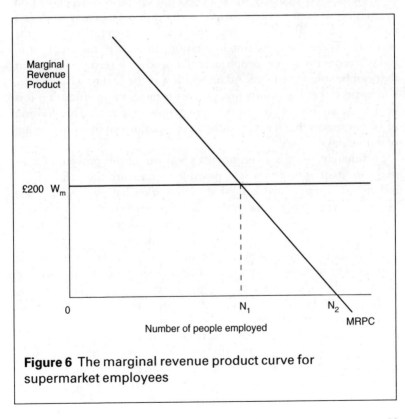

Figure 6 The marginal revenue product curve for supermarket employees

by the general supply and demand conditions prevailing in the market. In this case the market wage is established at point Wm, a rate of £200 per week. The rational employer would continue to employ workers as long as the value of the return on the last worker employed was greater than the cost i.e. their wage plus other add-on costs such as National Insurance and pension contributions. In this case it is worthwhile the employer continuing to take on workers up to the point N1. Up to that point each worker is worth more to the employer than it costs to employ them but beyond N1 extra workers are worth less. This analysis seems to make sense since which employers would take on people who they thought were not worth the outlay?

The position of the marginal revenue product curve is dependent on a number of factors. The value of a worker is affected by the amount of work done in a given time and the price attached to the output of the worker. This instantly raises problems. How much work does a supermarket worker do in a shift? Is it possible to measure the amount of work done particularly when a checkout operator is dependent on the number of customers coming through the doors and may work as a member of a team? Is there a price that can be put on the output of the workers? These are quite tough questions in view of the fact that in today's economy so few people actually produce a recognized output that can be sold for a price. **Adam Smith** was the first to write that he had noticed that the production process is much more efficient if it is broken down into small elements and people specialize. This **division of labour** means that it is very difficult to separate out the contribution of individual workers.

Fortunately, there is an economist's way out of this problem. *Let us make an assumption* that it is possible to measure the value of the individual output of workers, that each worker has exactly the same ability as every other worker, the output of each worker does have a price and the employer can employ as many workers as it wants at the market wage. Then the price of the goods or services produced multiplied by quantity of output produced will equal the value of the worker. The demand curve for workers will shift if either the price of the finished product or the output produced by each worker changes. The output will be affected by the effort put in by the worker, the skill the worker brings to the activity and also the amount of investment the employer pumps into the business to buy equipment that enables the worker to operate efficiently. In most cases where the value of an individual worker is difficult to calculate, the employer undertakes a job evaluation in order to set performance targets. They may well look at value in terms of what their competitors are paying or the employer could choose to link pay to the overall success of the company. If profits or turnover go up then the workforce has been more productive and could qualify for more pay. More companies are now adopting some form of **profit sharing** or bonus scheme to tie in the contribution of the individual employees with the wider success of the company. Directors in public companies are often paid in part by the issue of **share options** in the business where shares are allocated to them, which they can cash in if the share price rises. The directors then have an incentive to pursue policies that will boost share prices to give them the highest rewards.

Knowledge of the position of the marginal revenue product curve helps to determine how many people will be employed at the market wage but it does not explain why the wage was set at that level. For this we need to consider what is going on in the market for this kind of labour. The supply of a particular type of labour will be dependent on a number of factors. The higher the wage paid the more people will want to do a job causing a movement from one point on the supply curve to another.

Other factors will cause the supply curve to shift its position. A high level of skill, qualifications, length of training period or amount of experience required will cut down the potential number of applicants for a job. A change in the image associated with the career will affect supply. Often if a certain career becomes the centre of a television series that presents it in a favourable light, the numbers applying for that career shoot up. The growth of television programmes about animals and vets in practice has had the effect of pushing up the number of applicants to veterinary courses although police series have never seemed to have had the same effect. The working conditions and hours can affect supply. The move towards a 24-hour economy in the UK with more businesses open for longer hours has meant that more people are now expected to work unsociable hours as a normal part of their employment contract.

Employees will benefit if the supply of their labour is relatively inelastic i.e. the supply of workers does not change significantly even if the wage rises. This may be the situation faced by workers with particular skills such as doctors or where workers cannot be replaced by machines, such as accountants. People employed to produce goods with inelastic demand are likely to be safer in their jobs because the demand will remain more stable. Working for a monopoly supplier is always a good idea since their control of the market is likely to both create higher profits from which higher wages can be paid and more stable jobs.

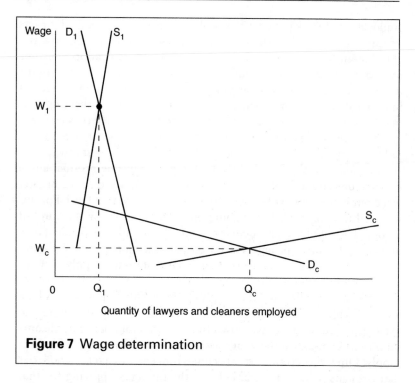

Figure 7 Wage determination

Figure 7 shows the way demand and supply interact in determining the wage paid. Lawyers with high demand (D1) and high value and with limited or inelastic supply (S1) will command high wages. Low value workers such as cleaners with a great supply (Sc) and relatively low value (Dc) will command low wages.

Some workers benefit from possessing a particular talent that is difficult or impossible to duplicate. Their supply cannot change. It is **perfectly inelastic.** As the demand for these workers increases so the demand curve shifts upwards but this can produce no increase in supply. The effect is that wage levels get pushed up and the worker earns well over what would be needed to keep that person in their existing line of work. Successful sportsmen and women, entertainers, film stars and business leaders can benefit from this and it explains why so many of them appear in the lists of the highest paid people. The amount that these wage stars could earn in their next best form of employment is known as their **transfer earnings** and any surplus over and above this is termed **economic rent.** However, as their popularity fades so their rent earnings will decrease.

Table 4 The high earners for 2000

The Top Ten Men	Annual Earnings
1 Bernie Eccleston – Son of a fisherman who now heads up Formula 1 Racing	£617m
2 John Hargreaves – Son of a Liverpool docker who part owns Matalan discount clothing stores	£237
3 Peter Harrison – Accountant and founder of computer network integration company Chernikeeff recently sold for £300m	£177m
4 John Duffield – Fund manager and venture capitalist sold his company to Commerzbank for £175m	£175m
5 Steve Morgan – Started off as a hod carrier but moved on to owning the building firm Redrow. Sold shares worth over £100m last year	£118m
6 Peter Kindersley – Started off as a sculptor but made money setting up a publishing firm with Christopher Dorling	£96m
7 David Hood – A television and hi-fi engineer who co-founded Pace Micro Technology which made satellite dishes and set-top boxes	£92m
8 Viscount Rothermere – Took over Associated Newspapers (publishers of the Mail) from his father. Highest earning representative of inherited wealth	£70m
9 David Potter – Founder of the Psion computer company	£66m
10 Philip Fleming – Son of family City Merchant Bank bought by Chase Manhatten	£65m

The Top Ten Women	
1 JK Rowling – Ex-teacher and creator of Harry Potter	£25m
2 Nikki Beckett – Founder of her own company NSB which supplies stock technology for retailers	£14m
3 The Queen – Income gained from the Civil List and the Privy Purse	£14m
4 Tracey Ullman – TV actress very big in the USA	£10m
5 Barbara Ward – Recently retired but was the Personnel Director of the Anglo-Dutch computer company CMG	£8.3m
6 Barbara-Taylor Bradford – The Yorkshire born writer has sold more than 60m novels	£7.4m
7 Jerry Hall – Model, actress and former wife of a Rolling Stone	£7.25m
8 Stephanie Powell – Recently won her money on the National Lottery	£7.1m
9 Jane Cavanagh – Founder of SCI Entertainment computer game company	£5.6m
10 Charlotte Church – At 15, the youngest person in the top ten. Singer from Cardiff	£5.5m

What do these tables reveal about payments to the highest paid workers?
Source: *The Sunday Times* Pay List 2000

The conclusion so far is that a person's wage is determined by the supply and demand conditions prevailing in the labour market in which the person is active. However, markets are rarely left to operate competitively. Employers attempt to exert monopoly power over the labour market just as they try to establish monopoly power in the product market. Individual workers lack power – they are dispensable as the business seeks to maximize profits. Their response has been to come together to form trade unions so that they can attempt to grab some power away from the employer. The unions also can act as pressure groups and try to influence government decisions. This role will be explored in the next chapter.

KEY WORDS

Industrial, occupational and geographic mobility of population
Derived demand
Marginal revenue product
Adam Smith

Division of labour
Profit sharing
Share options
Perfectly inelastic supply
Transfer earnings
Economic rent

Useful website
Globalization of Labour Markets – Greenway, Upward, Wright
www.nottingham.ac.uk/economics

Further reading
Davies, B., Hale, G., Smith, C., and Tiller, H., Chapter 2.9 in *Investigating Economics*, Macmillan, 1996.
Grant, S., Chapter 18 in Stanlake's *Introductory Economics*, 7th edn, Longman, 2000.
Grant, S., and Vidler, C., Part 2 Unit 6 in *Economics in Context*, Heinemann, 2000.
Griffiths, A., and Wall, S., (eds), Chapter 15 in *Applied Economics*, 8th edn, Longman, 1999.

Essay topics
1. (a) Distinguish between transfer earnings and economic rent.
   [8 marks]
   (b) Discuss what factors may cause a rise in the wage rate of teachers.
   [12 marks]

2. (a) How do economists use the concept of marginal revenue product to explain the demand for labour? [8 marks]
   (b) It was reported that the hourly wage rates of bus drivers in one part of the UK, fell from £7.90 in 1988 to £4.90 in 1996. Discuss the extent to which the concept of marginal revenue product can be used to explain this change. [12 marks]

Source: OCR, Q2, Paper 4387, June 1998.

Data response question
OCR, Q1, Paper 4387, November 2000.

What do they earn? What should they earn?

It is recognized that there is a serious recruitment crisis in some areas of the UK public sector, particularly in teaching and nursing. One reason may be that the public significantly underestimates what such workers are actually paid, and as a result the supply of new recruits is low. A recent Guardian/ICM opinion poll (conducted in January, 2000) asked what people think different jobs earn, and what they believe should be earned. The results are shown in Columns 1 and 2 of Figure 1 below. Column 3 shows the actual salaries of the average worker in each occupation.

On average, people in work earn about £20,000 per year. How much would you guess people in the following occupations earn per year? And how much do you think they ought to earn, on average, per year?

	What you think it is	What you think it ought to be	Actual earnings
Primary school teacher	18,700	22,000	22,511
Hospital porter	12,800	16,000	12,038
Ambulance staff	15,900	20,500	18,166
Nurse	16,000	23,000	19,200
Doctor	32,100	35,200	50,815
Senior civil servant	37,100	31,100	56,000 plus
Police officer	22,300	26,100	28,711
MP	47,800	32,500	47,008
Cabinet minister	71,600	43,400	94,157
University lecturer	34,600	33,000	32,000
Town hall staff (housing officer/librarian)	17,600	20,000	29,060

Figure 1
Source: *The Guardian*, 18 January, 2000 (adapted)

(a) (i) Which occupation does the public believe should obtain the largest pay rise? Explain your answer. [2 marks]

   (ii) Which occupation does the public believe is the most overpaid? [1 mark]

(b) Column 3 in Fig. 1 shows that the average university lecturer is paid well over twice the earnings of the average hospital porter. Use economic analysis to explain two likely reasons for this. [5 marks]

(c) (i) Explain briefly the meaning of 'transfer earnings'. [2 marks]

   (ii) To what extent can the concept be used to explain the fact that doctors sometimes become MPs? [5 marks]

(d) A 'recruitment crisis' implies a shortage of supply relative to demand at the current rate of pay. Discuss the suggestion that the recruitment crisis for public-sector nurses might be caused by under-estimation by the public of what nurses actually earn. [5 marks]

Chapter Three

Labour markets and market failure

'Join the union and together say Equal Pay for Equal Work.'
Susan B. Anthony, 1869

The assumptions required, if the free market model is to be useful in explaining what we see around us in the labour market, are rarely found in practice. The point about leaving decisions to markets is that, with no government intervention, they will lead to resources being employed efficiently in ways that create the maximum level of welfare for the people of the country. Ideally we should be looking for a situation where it is impossible to create more welfare by redistributing any of the country's labour from one use to another. Does the market method of determining wages produce this outcome? This is highly debateable.

What happens if the assumptions do not hold? Free market supporters would advocate that we should develop a system that matches the ideal as closely as possible. Markets should be opened up to free competition and any barriers to this should be removed. But markets can lead to imperfect outcomes. Market failure occurs. Markets are not a neutral set of arrangements free from any values or bias. They favour the rich and economically powerful. The poor and weak will not benefit and are likely to get poorer and weaker. **Income inequality** and **poverty** results and these will be discussed in Chapter 7.

Two major forms of market failure will be examined here. The first looks at sex, race or age discrimination and discrimination against the disabled present in the UK economy. The second looks at the power structure within the labour market and the role of trade unions.

Discrimination

It would be good to think that all recruitment, promotion, wage and other decisions at work are made on the basis of rational thought and argument. Unfortunately, this is not the case. We are all influenced by our own prejudices, likes and dislikes to some extent but there is potential danger if these are allowed to impact too heavily on the labour market. One estimate is that up to half of all pay inequality is due to discrimination. One result of **sex discrimination** has been the long-term gap between male and female earnings. It took over 100 years after Susan Anthony's plea to get The Equal Pay Act which has now been in force for over 30 years and the Sex Discrimination Act for over 25 years. It would be reasonable to think that by this time equal pay should no longer be an issue but the statistics prove otherwise. In 1970 women's hourly pay averaged 63% of men's and by 2000 the figure had risen to 80.9%. Over a working life this means that, on average, a woman would earn £240,000 less than a man and £380,000 if the woman had had two children. If we look at gross weekly earnings, which include overtime pay, the figures look worse with full-time female employees earning 72% of the men's wage. One difficulty is that employment is often divided between jobs that are either male or female dominated making comparison difficult. Women have also been pushed into part-time work which usually commands lower pay rates. But even when men and women are employed in the same occupation, men's earnings are always higher. Nurses, care assistants, secretaries, cleaners and clerks are occupations dominated by female employment with about 80% of employees being women but they are also relatively poorly paid. Women are also not well represented in higher paid jobs or at higher management levels. **Glass ceilings** exist with only five of the country's 100 largest companies having women on their boards. The situation for women in the UK is not the worst in Europe. In Portugal, the Netherlands and Greece women receive poorer treatment with the pay gap being even higher.

The market does provide an answer to the problem. If women are discriminated against then the pay of women will fall well below that of men. Eventually the pay differential will make it worthwhile for companies to employ fewer men and more women. At this point men's wages will begin to fall and women's wages begin to catch up. In the long run the wage differential between men and women will reduce, but how long will it take and should society accept this prejudicial, irrational attitude towards a key group of people? The market needs to be reminded that such treatment is wrong and it needs some controls put in place to achieve the optimum use of resources.

Discrimination in the labour market also occurs between racial groups. The situation is symbolized by a recent **race discrimination** court case faced by Microsoft in the USA. In 2001 only 2.6% of the company's 21,429 employees were black and black staff made up only 1.6% of the managerial staff compared with 13% of the total population. This situation is typically also found in the UK. The **McPherson Report** into policing following the murder of the black teenager, Stephen Lawrence, identified the existence of what was termed 'institutional racism'. This was defined as 'The collective failure of an organization to provide an appropriate and professional service to people because of their colour, culture or ethnic origin. It can be seen or detected in processes, attitudes and behaviour which amount to discrimination through unwitting prejudice, ignorance, thoughtlessness and racist stereotyping which disadvantage minority ethnic people'. It is undoubtedly the case that many institutions in the UK display such characteristics which work to the disadvantage of certain groups. In economic terms the effects of tolerating discrimination are to accept an unfair economic system and to under-use scarce resources which therefore diminishes the living standards of us all.

Age discrimination is of growing concern. With the decline in the birth rate and the fact that people are living longer, the numbers of people moving into the over-50 age group is increasing. Between 1990 and 1999 this group increased by 755,000 but the participation rate has been in decline. For men the participation rate has fallen from 80% for the 60–65 age group to 50% in the last 20 years. For the 55–59 age group it has fallen from 90% to 75%. In other words, large numbers of older men have been dropping out of the workforce. For women the situation has been the reverse with a growing percentage of older women staying in the workforce. This can be partly explained by the changing structure of the labour market with more jobs being created in the service sector (more female dominated) and continued decline in the traditional male employment areas such as manufacturing. Companies have tried to reduce the size of their workforces by substituting younger, cheaper workers for older workers. Older workers have been encouraged to leave by the offer of enhanced redundancy packages or through the granting of long-term sick leave. Once out of the workforce these people may struggle to get back in as they lose skills and touch with working life. Again, the loss of a group of experienced workers means that a considerable resource is not being used and output levels suffer.

There are estimated to be over 8 million people in the UK who have some form of physical or mental disability. Their rights are protected under the **Disability Discrimination** Act of 1995 and the Disability Rights Commission set up in 1999. Without some protection it is clear that this group would be subject to prejudiced treatment. In this case an Act of Parliament helps to shape attitudes, guarantee fair treatment and ensure that valuable economic resources are used to their full potential.

Enabling the disabled

A 400,000-strong pool of talent is fit and ready to work. So, asks **Jim Pollard**, why aren't these people in jobs?

Only a handful of employers have been prosecuted for discriminating against disabled people in the entire three-and-a-half years since the Disability Discrimination Act made this illegal. The Disability Rights Commission, established three months ago by the Government to give the Act more teeth, has backed one case all the way to the court.

Three million of the 5.2 million disabled Britons of working age have jobs, but about 400,000 more are willing and able to work. Britain lags behind countries such as Holland in protecting the rights of the disabled to hold down a job.

Progress has been made in the UK in the past couple of decades: more disabled people have the confidence to seek work; discrimination has been outlawed, and there has been a raft of Government initiatives aimed at improving the situation. So who needs more help?

Writer Penny Pepper, for one. She was put into an institution as a child; her life was run by doctors. It was assumed that she was unlikely to leave. Now in her thirties, she lives independently with her husband, who is also disabled. They receive help under national and local authority independent living schemes to meet their care needs, but the couple control how the money is spent.

So far so good. But, says Pepper: 'I'd like to work but can't. Definitions are too rigid, and because I can't work much of the time, I'm registered as incapable. In fact, with a bit of flexibility, I could work. I can write and I know there are organisations who would offer me work because they have done so in the past.

'The other problem is the benefits trap. Under independent living schemes you can only earn a certain amount. As a result disabled people find themselves working twice as hard for half as much.'

According to the DRC, there are more than 2.6 million disabled people out of work and, like Pepper, a million of them would like to work if they could.

The Minister for Disabled People, Margaret Hodge, believes the 400,000 can be freed to get jobs if the Government tackles the 'huge issue' of the Access To Work scheme, under which disabled workers and their employers can receive financial and practical support.

'The figures are horrendous,' Hodge says. 'Disabled people are six times more likely to be unemployed than non-disabled people. Work is a civil right for disabled people. When I took over this job it surprised me that it wasn't seen as such. We're trying to speed up Access to Work.'

But the Minister stresses that the scheme aims to help employers meet their legal obligations, rather than enable them to be benevolent. 'Employers have an obligation to make reasonable adjustment for disabled staff.'

The New Deal for Disabled People is not like such schemes for other groups, she says. 'It's as much about breaking down employers' prejudices. We want to look at contracting specialist brokers to match disabled people with vacancies.'

The Sunday Observer, 6 August 2000

Trade unions

In a Capitalist system it is the owners of capital who have the economic power. They employ people to produce goods and services which are sold for profit. The workforce is paid for its efforts but any surplus value is creamed off as a return on the capital employed. To boost profit there is an inevitable clash of interests as employers (or bourgeoisie) try to keep wages low and the workers (or proletarians) push for wage increases. This conflict of purpose led Karl Marx as a final statement in the *Communist Manifesto* to call for the 'WORKING MEN OF ALL COUNTRIES, UNITE!' against these forces. His view was that the value of any product was dependent on the value of the labour which had gone into its production: a **Labour Theory of Value**. No production can take place without labour and so the labour element of production should receive all of the rewards. In taking their profit, Capitalists were seizing what was, rightfully, the workers'.

Few today would fully accept Marx's ideas on value but the divisions between employer and employee still exist. One response of the workforce has been to form trade unions to represent the interests of different groups of workers. A trade union is legally defined as 'an organization which consists wholly or mainly of workers of one or more descriptions and whose principal purposes include the regulation of relations between workers and employers'. Traditionally the role of trade unions has been to engage in the process of collective bargaining to negotiate to improve the pay and conditions of employment of their members. Their work is much wider than this, advising on employment rights, health and safety, discrimination, human rights, lifelong learning and training issues. Unions provide legal advice, represent members in tribunals and supply a range of other financial and welfare-related services. They act as a pressure group to get changes in the law to benefit their members. For example, they have strongly supported the introduction of a National Minimum Wage and the unions' close relationship with the Labour Party has helped to secure some of the changes they would have wanted.

Trade union activities are controlled by a body of law brought together in the Trade Union and Labour Relations (Consolidation) Act 1992 which covers their organizational procedure and their rights. In the UK everybody has a right to join a trade union but, equally, people can choose not to join. Legislation in the 1980s and 90s restricted the ability of unions to take industrial action and the changing structure of industry and rising unemployment of that period caused union membership to decline. From 1987–97 membership fell from 10.4 million to 7.8 million. However, perhaps double this number are covered by union-negotiated agreements which means that millions of people gain some of the benefit of union membership without paying their dues. Some of these 'free riders' may be coming back into the union fold because in the last couple of years there has been a small recovery in membership.

Official strikes, for which a ballot has been held, rarely take place in industrial disputes today and unofficial ones, or 'wildcat' strikes are illegal. In 1998 there were only 166 stoppages, the lowest number since 1891 and the working days lost in industrial action in the 1990s have been below 400,000 (in the General Strike of 1926 over 160 million working days were lost). This does not mean that the right to strike is not important. The fact that a union may be balloting its members on industrial action shows their serious intent and often concentrates the minds of negotiators to produce an agreement. Unions represent a wide spectrum of people ranging from the Military and Orchestral Musical Instrument Makers Trade Society (MOMIMTS) with 57 members to UNISON which draws its 1,272,330 members mainly from the public sector. In some workplaces employees can be represented by a number of different unions and, in the past, this did give rise to demarcation or who-does-what disputes. Unions are still fiercely protective of their membership but modern employers increasingly try to arrange single union agreements to avoid inter-union problems and make the communication process easier. Some of these so-called 'sweet heart' deals are criticized because the union may surrender its right to strike to secure its special relationship with the employer. However, the recent labour relations record suggests that there is much to be gained from harmonious industrial relations.

What are the economic effects of trade unions?
If it is impossible to precisely measure the value of a particular group of employees then value becomes a matter of opinion and an issue for discussion. It is in the employers' interests to undervalue the contribution of employees whilst unions may seek to talk up that value. There is some evidence from Workplace Employee Relations Surveys that unionized workplaces do result in greater productivity and more training which would support unions' arguments that employees are worth more. Through collective bargaining, agreement is eventually reached and a wage settlement agreed. Unions may also attempt to reduce the supply of labour by maintaining certain controls on the numbers of new recruits. This may be done by supporting the retention of a lengthy training period, as in the law and accountancy, or insisting on union membership before somebody can enter a job, for example, the acting profession. The effects of trade union action are shown in Figure 8.

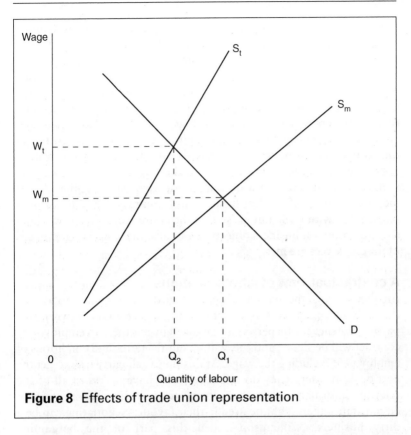

Figure 8 Effects of trade union representation

In Figure 8 the free market wage would be Wm. The effect of trade union action is to force up the wage to Wt but this means that less people will be employed at the higher wage.

Trade union intervention in a labour market can have the effect of separating the market into two: the unionized sector with high wages and good working conditions and the non-unionized sector with a higher supply of labour and worse pay and working conditions. The split is between **insiders and outsiders** with unions protecting their own members' interests whilst calling on the government to support the needs of the outsiders. In Figure 8 Q2 Q1 extra workers would have been employed in this occupation if wage determination had been left freely to the labour market. But these people now have to look for work elsewhere and so the supply for other jobs increases. This raises the wages in the unionized sector but depresses the wage level in the non-unionized sector.

There is an argument that employers can also benefit from a unionized workforce. Hirschmann's (1970) **'exit'/'voice' theory** suggested that there could be financial gains. If employees have grievances, they have basically two choices: they can raise the issue with management i.e. they can talk about it and get the problem sorted out, or they can quit the employer. If employees left at every dispute, then employers would be faced with high costs associated with a high labour turnover. There would be recruitment costs, training costs and the costs of lost production. By having an effective communication system, which trade unions can assist, these costs are saved, a stable workforce is achieved and output, productivity and profitability is increased. Some of the most successful companies try to achieve partnership with trade unions so that the entire workforce is working towards common business objectives but also the concerns and needs of the employees are met.

A contractual view of labour relations

An alternative to the market model of wage determination is to look at the wage setting process as an act of forming a contract between two parties. Whenever one person is employed by another, an employment contract will be signed and this will set out the terms and conditions of employment including the wage. At this time each party tries to get the best deal on offer. They do not necessarily have access to all of the relevant information but they do try to make use of any fact or circumstance that might be used in their favour. Negotiating can be a dirty business. Williamson called this part of the bargaining **'opportunism'**. Parties also need to make best use of any leverage they might have. A union can bring the leverage of the support of a large number of employees or the threat of some form of industrial action; a sports star seeking to sponsor products might raise the prospect of going to a competitor. Gorringe called these costs incurred if the contract negotiations fail: **'hostages'**. The outcome of any wage negotiation then becomes subject to the balance of opportunism and hostages. In other words, this theory suggests that brute economic power and cunning, rather than the forces of supply and demand, determines the wage.

Would you pay £5m for this space?

German firm DVAG yesterday agreed to pay Michael Schumacher more than £5m to fill this 10cm red space on his Ferrari Cap from next season.

The Guardian, 8 November 1999

KEY WORDS

Income inequality	Disability discrimination
Poverty	Trade unions
Sex discrimination	Labour theory of value
Glass ceilings	Insiders and outsiders
Race discrimination	Exit/voice theory
McPherson report	Opportunism
Age discrimination	Hostages

Useful websites

www.wsws.org.articles
A Contracting Theory View of Industrial Relations – Peter Gorringe
   www.hrnicholls.com
Equal Opportunities Commission www.eoc.org.uk
Equal Pay Task Force www.bt.com/equalpaytaskforce/
Commission for Racial Equality www.cre.gov.uk
Trades Union Congress www.tuc.org.uk

Further reading

Anderton, A., Units 73, 74 and 75 in *Economics*, 3rd edn, Causeway Press, 2000.

Grant, S., Chapter 22 in Stanlake's *Introductory Economics*, 7th edn, Longman, 2000.

Grant, S., and Vidler, C., Part 2 Unit 7 in *Economics in Context*, Heinemann, 2000.

Munday, S., Chapters 1–4 in *Markets and Market Failure*, Heinemann Educational, 2000.

Karl Marx and Friedrich Engels, *The Communist Manifesto*, Oxford Paperbacks, 1998.

Your rights at work – a TUC Guide, Kagan Page, 2000.

Essay topics

1. (a) Explain what is meant by labour market failure.   [8 marks]
   (b) Discuss the effects of gender discrimination on the operation of labour markets.   [12 marks]
2. Relative wages may depend on demand and supply, but the nature of the industry in which workers are employed has at least as much influence.
   (a) Explain what determines the demand for labour in a perfectly competitive labour market.   [10 marks]
   (b) With reference to the market for manual workers in an industry such as car assembly, discuss the extent to which the level of wages may differ from that determined in a perfectly competitive market.   [15 marks]

Source: OCR, Q2, Specimen Paper 2884, 2000.

Data response question
Edexcel, Q2, Paper 3, June 1997.

Figure 1 Full and part-time employment, UK: by sex (thousands)

Year	Males		Females	
	Full-time	Part-time	Full-time	Part-time
1984	13,240	570	5,422	4,343
1985	13,336	575	5,503	4,457
1986	13,430	647	5,662	4,566
1987	13,472	750	5,795	4,696
1988	13,881	801	6,069	4,808
1989	14,071	734	6,336	4,907
1990	14,109	789	6,479	4,928
1991	13,686	799	6,350	4,933
1992	13,141	885	6,244	5,081
1993	12,769	886	6,165	5,045
1994	12,875	998	6,131	5,257

(Source: *Social Trends*, 1995, HMSO)

Figure 2 Changes in working population by sector, UK (percentages)

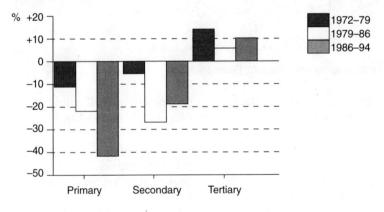

(Source: *Dataset*, Trigon Press, 1995)

Figure 3 Union membership in UK, 1980–1994

Figure 4 Number of strikes, UK 1976–95

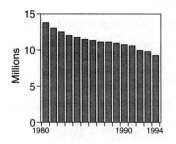

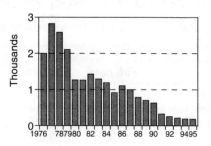

(Source: Central Statistical Office)

(Source: *Dataset*, Trigon Press, 1995)

Figure 5 Average growth in real earnings, UK, 1976–93

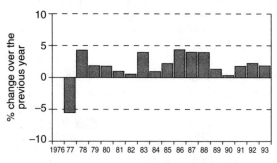

(Source: *Employment Gazette*, February 1995)

(a) (i) Using Figure 1, calculate the proportion of total employment accounted for by part-time employees in both 1984 and 1994.

[3 marks]

    (ii) Suggest reasons why employers have offered an increasing number of part-time employment opportunities. [4 marks]

(b) (i) With reference to Figure 1, compare the changes in male and female employment since 1984. [3 marks]

    (ii) With reference to Figures 1 and 2, how might the changes in female employment be explained? [6 marks]

(c) To what extent do the data suggest that there has been a decline in the influence of trade unions? [6 marks]

(d) Examine one other factor, apart from the power of trade unions, which might affect real wages. [3 marks]

Chapter Four

Government intervention

'The old arguments about government are now outdated big against small, interventionist against laissez-faire.'
Tony Blair, PM UK, White Paper on Modernizing Government, 1999.

A free labour market has its strengths. It rations out the available labour supplies with those in greatest demand earning the highest wages. It provides signals to the workforce so that the supply of labour is increased to shortage areas and moves away from jobs where there is no longer a demand. The system is efficient in that there is no direct cost of joining, and fair in that the market could be said to be neutral in its values. No one group is able to control the market.

Free markets, however, do have their problems. Their outcomes may not provide society with the optimum use of resources; markets may fail. The main forms of market failure arise from the lack of perfect information available to participants, the lack of labour mobility, the wage inequality that results in free labour markets, the exercise of monopoly power in the market and the external effects of decisions made in the labour market. Should these factors lead to some economic inefficiency and a misallocation of scarce resources, the government could choose to intervene in order to correct any perceived market failure. Different types of intervention will be needed to respond to different forms of market failure. Despite the Prime Minister's view, there is still a debate about the degree to which governments should intervene in the economy and the scale of the role governments should play.

Lack of perfect information
To make rational economic choices people need access to perfect information. In the labour market, this is very difficult. Job vacancies are advertised in a number of places including at the place of employment, in local and national newspapers and the specialist press, from private employment or recruitment agencies and the job centres. Individuals are never sure that they are in command of the complete picture. Jobs will pay different wages and benefits, have different working conditions and job descriptions, different career prospects and different locations. Comparisons are inevitably difficult and to complicate matters further, only a limited range of employers are seeking new people at any one time.

Perfect information seems elusive. The government can make some impact by providing a comprehensive service and support from the Employment Service which will advertise posts widely geographically and assist people claiming jobseekers' allowance to keep in touch with the job market. Appropriate training can be provided in basic employability skills, such as completing application forms and producing CVs. Local Employment Service offices can build up comprehensive knowledge of the local job market and so can offer good quality employment advice and provide information about any government schemes. They can identify skill shortages and attempt to encourage training in those areas. The government may also develop assistance for training which will lead to a better match between the demand and supply of work-based skills. Individual Learning Accounts are one example of recent government innovation to subsidize any employees who want to get back into training. In the longer term, the government may try to change the schools curriculum to increase the amount of vocational education undertaken.

Perhaps the biggest contributor to improving the information available to the workforce is the growing use of the Internet as a notice board for job vacancies. This medium is by far the easiest to manage from the job applicant's point of view and it does give the chance for the applicant to survey the job scene. As more employers make use of the Internet the market will approach much more closely the ideal of perfect information.

Lack of labour mobility

In a free market, resources should be free to move around to where they are most needed. This can be difficult in the UK. It is widely known that wages in London are higher than in other parts of the country so, in theory, workers should flock to London away from low wage areas. To some extent London is a draw for young professionals but many simply are not able to make the move. The prices of houses in London are very high and many people may not wish to move away from friends and family. The government may be able to do something here by making low cost housing available to people wanting to move to the capital, improving transport connections, subsidizing interview costs and re-location expenses.

The issue of mobility is important when considering the UK's membership of the **Single European Market**. Essential to this market are the four freedoms: the freedom of movement of goods, services, capital and people. If one country is experiencing labour shortages and wages are rising while another country is experiencing unemployment, it should be possible for labour to flow from one country to the other without restriction. If labour is immobile within a country, it will be less mobile between countries where there are additional problems of language and distance. If there were to be large flows of people between countries there could follow increased racial tensions between different groups and the associated problems.

Wage inequality

A free market will tend to lead to unequal incomes. Those who possess rare skills or talents that are in great demand will be able to command high wages but people with poor basic skills may experience very low wages or unemployment. The problem with wages is that they are not just a price; they provide the means by which a family is able to live. Businesses can, in their search for profit, exploit some employees and pay them poverty wages. It is not a fair system.

The government is able to use a number of strategies to even out some of the excesses of the free market. **Fiscal policy** covers the use of public expenditure and taxation to solve the problem. A major source of revenue for the government is **direct taxes** or taxes on income. In the UK income tax is a **progressive tax** in that those on high incomes pay tax at a greater percentage rate than those on lower incomes. People are allowed to earn the first part of their income free of tax. The next portion of income is taxed at 10%, the next portion 22% and then income earned over £32,385 (in 2001 assuming the taxpayer claims no other allowances) is taxed at 40%. These rates will change depending on the tax strategy followed by the Chancellor of the Exchequer and Prime Minister. The system is far less progressive than it was 20 years ago. When Mrs Thatcher and the Conservatives came to power in 1979, the top rate of tax was 83% and so it seems that we have become kinder to the high wage earners over the years. Also the burden of taxation has shifted to indirect taxes such as VAT and petrol duty. These are **indirect taxes** placed on expenditure and are **regressive** in that they charge each person the same amount of tax on the goods they buy but this represents a higher proportion of the low income-earner's wage. The result was that the gap between rich and poor widened during the 1980s and 90s.

The other side of the public sector is the benefits paid to support lower income groups. Examples of these are pensions paid to those over retirement age, jobseekers' allowance paid to the unemployed, maternity and sick pay and child benefit: a flat rate benefit paid to families with children under the age of 16. Governments face a choice of providing these benefits as means tested i.e. related to the income of the recipient or flat rate and paid to everyone who qualifies. Means tested benefits seem to target money more effectively but have a lower take-up rate and so may not get to the people most in need. These benefits directly boost the incomes of the poor but benefits are also provided in kind. State education and the health service come free of direct charge and their effect is to provide additional help to the poor.

All is not perfect. It is still possible for people to avoid paying taxes through the employment of a good accountant, offshore tax havens or the hidden cash economy. In recent years the distribution of income has become more unequal due to the high pay increases awarded to the already well paid. There may be some advantages of this. The American economist, Laffer, has strongly argued that if a society wants to encourage enterprise it must reward it. Lower tax rates at the top end provide the incentive for people to work harder, create jobs and stay to pay their taxes in the country. The world has become more tax competitive with countries enticing businesses to them by the prospect of low tax rates. There is some debate about Laffer's ideas but it provides an attractive argument to any government looking for free market solutions to problems and wanting to woo the electorate with a promise of tax cuts.

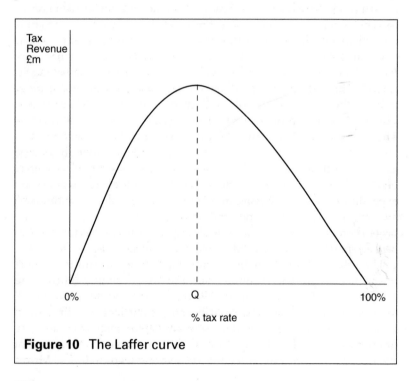

Figure 10 The Laffer curve

The Laffer curve shown in Figure 10 illustrates the theoretical effects of imposing different rates of tax on the amount of tax revenue raised by the Government. At 0% tax rates zero revenue is raised. As the tax rate rises so the amount of revenue increases but only does so up to a point. If tax rates are raised above level Q then the tax raised begins to fall. Eventually, if tax rates are 100% there is no incentive to earn any money since it all will be taken in tax. At high rates of tax it is likely that people will try harder to find ways around paying tax and may even leave the country for low tax havens. A key question is at what level does Q appear? In the UK the highest tax rate on income is 40% – is this too high or is it too low? The Laffer curve gives little guidance.

A government also needs to look to its **macro-economic management** if it wishes to close the income gap. One of the biggest causes of inequality is the number of families with no major breadwinner. If the government tolerates high unemployment there will be greater division between those in work and those without. Reducing unemployment reduces income inequality. The government can deploy a range of aggregate demand and supply side policies to boost the economy. Details of the different approaches will be given in Chapter 5.

Incomes policies appear to have become far less fashionable today than in the 1970s. The idea is that the government, if it so wished, could control the level of pay increases given. This could be done either voluntarily or with legal compulsion. For example, wage rises could be set at a fixed percentage rate, for example, 3%, a fixed amount of money e.g. £100 per month or index-linked to price rises. This would seem to produce a fair system since everybody would be bound by the same rules. The problem is that such controls have never been successfully introduced in the UK over the long term. Governments have used them to try to control excessive pay rises and they have worked for a time but, after the removal of controls, the floodgates open and wages resumed their upward path. If the government does control wage levels then wages are not being allowed to perform their role in a free market of rationing and signalling shortages to the rest of the economy.

It may, therefore, look as if incomes policies have been consigned to the economic scrap heap. However, this conclusion would be wrong. The government and the Bank of England always keep a watchful brief over the general levels of pay increase. They are never afraid to spell out the dangers of wages rising too fast and will often apply pressure to keep pay raises and inflation in check. Any signs that pay is beginning to rise too fast and the economic brakes are applied in the form of an interest rate rise. It therefore appears that the country is in the grip of a permanent incomes policy targeting average pay increases. The benefit of this approach is that the mirage of a free market is maintained and the government is not drawn into the difficult area of trying to fix wage increases themselves.

The **National Minimum Wage** was introduced in 1998. This set a basic minimum wage rate below which nobody could be paid. Initially the rate set was £3.60 per hour for workers over the age of 21 and this has been up-rated to £4.10. The rates are set on the advice of the Low Pay Commission. The Government argued that the NMW protected employees against exploitative employers and gave workers much greater self-respect instead of having to rely on state benefits. In particular, it helped a lot of part-time workers, many of whom are women, and so contributed to reducing the gap between male and female earnings. The argument against was the fear that many of the low paid workers would now be sacked because their marginal product revenue would not be worth the higher level of pay, low profit-making small firms would not be able to afford to pay and it would lead to higher unemployment. Given a choice, would people prefer to be in work but receive a low wage or be unemployed but with a NMW? With up to 2 million people potentially affected by the NMW, there could

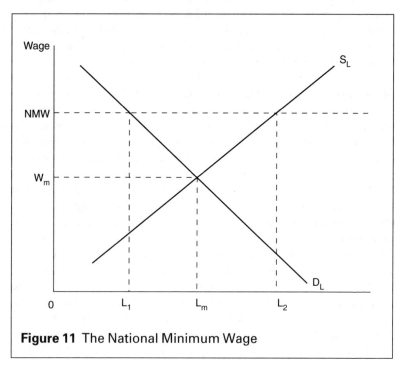

Figure 11 The National Minimum Wage

have been a substantial increase in unemployment. In the event, no such increase occurred. The effect of the introduction of the NMW is shown in Figure 11.

In Figure 11, in the free labour market the equilibrium wage would be set at Wm where the supply of labour equals the demand for labour and there is no unemployment. If the National Minimum Wage is introduced at level NMW then there is an extension of supply because more people are now attracted to employment and a contraction of demand since employers wish to take on fewer workers at the higher wage level. Unemployment equal to L1 L2 should be the result. But such unemployment did not materialize. Why not? There are four possible explanations. First, employers were previously exploiting their workers by paying them below their value measured in terms of marginal revenue product. Being forced to pay a higher wage reduces the employer's profits. Second, employers kept workers on and absorbed the increase in costs out of their profits. This would have been much easier for businesses if the Minimum Wage were fixed at a relatively low level. Evidence since its introduction suggests that this was the case. Thirdly, the employers demanded an increase in productivity from the low paid workers since they were now costing more: the efficiency wage argument. Fourth, it might have been the case that the introduction of the NMW coincided with an upturn in the economy which boosted the demand for labour and so reduced any negative impact the NMW might have had on employment.

Monopoly power in the labour market

The existence of monopolies in a market distorts the allocation of resources. Monopolists try to restrict the supply of their goods or services in order to push up price. The same pressures are at work in the labour market. Single buyers of some types of labour, or **monopsonists**, may develop in certain parts of the country such as Nissan in Washington, County Durham or Toyota in Derbyshire and the presence of these companies will distort the local labour market. Other firms drawing labour from the same area will have to raise their wages to prevent labour from drifting away and local house prices will rise. This prosperity may be fine whilst the business is booming but causes a problem when market conditions change and the business needs to downsize. As companies shed labour, unemployment black spots are created. Cutbacks from major companies such as BMW, General Motors and Corus the steel manufacturers, have heaped social problems on the Midlands, Luton and South Wales. Public sector organizations such as the National Health Service, the Police

49

Authorities, the Local Education Authorities and Social Services are also, largely, single buyers. The value of employees in these sectors is difficult to determine precisely, and the employers therefore have greater power to fix wage levels since there is no equivalent free market value.

On the supply side, trade unions built up their strength on their ability to control certain groups of workers. By achieving **monopoly supply**, unions were able to negotiate on more equal terms with employers and force through higher wages and better working conditions. Legislation in the 1980s weakened their position. The closed shop where employees had to join particular trade unions to gain work has effectively been abolished and the restrictions on picketing and strikes have weakened union power. Some professional associations such as the British Medical Association and the Law Society do retain the power to strike off individuals from the official lists of practitioners and also have some control over the professional examinations. The government has taken some action to break down these institutional monopolies by opening up the careers to greater competition, for example, by breaking down the barriers between barristers and solicitors.

The external effects of labour market decisions

Decisions about wages affect more than just the workers involved. They have a wider impact on the economy. If wages are rising, then the level of aggregate demand in the economy will be rising. This could be creating jobs and reducing unemployment but it could also be generating inflation. Inflation hits at the living standards of all of us since it destroys the value of money and means that we can buy less with our pounds. During the 1970s, 1980s and 1990s the control of inflation was deemed to be the number one priority of successive governments so wage decisions could not be completely free market driven.

What happens to wages has an important impact on the economy of particular parts of the country. Wage rises in London and the South East have a ripple effect on other regions. In Devon, Cornwall and Norfolk, for example, the housing market is greatly affected by people moving out from the capital. Having sold high priced houses in London, people are able to scoop up the relatively cheaper properties in the other regions distorting the housing market there. The second home market has the effect of making houses in these areas too expensive for locals and destroying the life of villages. Some response may be needed from the government if the rural lifestyle is to survive. This could come in the form of housing subsidies for local people or measures to remove Council Tax concessions which would make second home purchase more expensive.

Government failure

Up to this point the government has been depicted as an all-knowing, beneficial influence on the economy only intervening when it sees market failure emerging. But government intervention carries risks. Whenever the government intervenes in order to correct some aspect of perceived market failure, the outcome in terms of the efficient use of resources could be worse than if the market was allowed to operate unhindered. It may be relatively easy to identify where the market is making mistakes but it is much more difficult to determine the exact nature of the required intervention. If the government does get the decision wrong and the welfare of the economy suffers then the economy is experiencing **government failure**.

Governments are not neutral. They don't act like a referee at a football match. They have their own agenda to push through, their own set of principles to guide policy, their own backers to please and their own self-interest. **Public Choice Theory** arising from the work of James Buchanan and Gordon Tullock attempts to explain the process of public decision-making. Governments ideally look for decisions where the benefits go to the many and the costs are borne by the few because this will be in their political interest making them more likely to be re-elected at the next election. Many Labour supporters have been disappointed with the record of the government in that it does not seem to have followed a strongly Socialist agenda. The government's view has been that its longer term political survival will be assured if it manages to convince a wider section of society to vote for it at the next election and it has chosen to do this by offering a relatively middle-of-the-road set of actions to which few can object. Although higher taxes on the rich would seem an easy way to address income inequality, the government is reluctant to do it because they fear that these people carry considerable weight and influence and should not be offended.

Government ministers earn their money through having to make these difficult judgments but such intervention opens up areas for political debate. It is undoubtedly the case that governments did get things wrong when introducing incomes policies during the 1970s. Linking wages to the inflation rate added to inflationary pressure rather than reduce it. The net welfare of the country suffered as a result. Government decisions to keep a tight lid on public sector pay increases in the period following the general election in 1997 meant that pay

Limits eased on foreign teachers

WILL WOODWARD EDUCATION EDITOR

The government took further steps to lift recruitment problems in schools yesterday by making it easier for foreign teachers to work in England.

Until now teachers from countries outside the European economic area, including South Africa, Australia and New Zealand, could work in English schools for a maximum of two years.

Estelle Morris, the school standards minister, extended the time limit to four years. She also removed a rule which meant those teachers could work in the same school for only four months.

"Our proposals will cut through bureaucracy to ensure that where schools have recruited overseas teachers they benefit from the skills and experience they have to offer," Ms Morris said.

Several hundred, possibly thousands, of teachers from Commonwealth countries are teaching in the UK – though no figures are held centrally.

If teachers from those countries want to teach in England for longer than four years they need to obtain an English teaching qualification. But Ms Morris said the teacher training agency was considering making the process quicker.

Nigel de Gruchy, general secretary of the National Association of Schoolmasters Union of Women Teachers, said "It's a small step which could help in the short term but this over-reliance on foreign supply teachers is dangerous. It is more reminiscent of a developing country than the world's fourth largest economy."

The Observer, 20 January 2001

levels fell below those in the private sector. This led to recruitment difficulties and shortages of teachers, doctors, nurses, midwives and social workers. The market solution would be to raise wages but the government has tried to boost supply by easing the restrictions on foreign workers with the demanded skills, giving golden hellos to trainees, increasing advertising and trying to persuade people who have left these professions to return.

Given all the uncertainties and inconsistencies of government action and the fact that government values are strongly influenced by a variety of supporters' interest groups leads some people to keep faith with the market. The size and scope of government intervention in the economy forms one of the great economic and political divides.

> **KEY WORDS**
>
> Labour mobility   Macro-economic management
> Single European Market   Incomes policies
> Fiscal policy   National Minimum Wage
> Direct taxes   Monopsonists
> Progressive tax   Monopoly supply
> Indirect taxes   Government failure
> Regressive tax   Public Choice Theory
> Laffer curve

Useful websites

Introduction to Public Choice Theory – Leon Felkins
  www.magnolia.net
Public Choice Theory: An Introduction – Julie Novak
  www.cis.org.au/Policy
Rent-Seeking, Public Choice, and the Prisoner's Dilemma
  www.friesian.com
The website of the Low Pay Unit www.lowpay.gov.uk

Further reading

Atkinson, B., Livesey, F., and Milward, R., Chapter 8 in *Applied Economics*, Macmillan, 1998.

Grant, S., Chapter 24 in Stanlake's *Introductory Economics*, 7th edn, Longman, 2000.

Grant, S., and Vidler, C., Part 2 Unit 8 in *Economics in Context*, Heinemann, 2000.

Munday, S., Chapters 4–7 in *Markets and Market Failure*, Heinemann Educational, 2000.

Essay topics

1. (a) Explain the causes of a lack of labour mobility.   [10 marks]
   (b) Discuss measures a government could take to promote labour mobility.   [10 marks]

2. (a) Explain the effect that monopsonists and monopolists can have on the operation of labour markets.   [10 marks]
   (b) Assess the impact of a national minimum wage on the efficiency of labour markets.   [10 marks]

Data response question
OCR, Q1, Paper 4387, June 2000.

A National Minimum Wage

In May 1998, the government-appointed Low Pay Commission (LPC) produced its first report. Amongst its recommendations was that there should be a National Minimum Wage (NMW) of £3.60 per hour.

The introduction of a NMW in the UK is argued by the LPC to be 'a major initiative to address **in-work poverty** and promote **work incentives**. It should also bring a range of further benefits, including greater equality in pay between the sexes and between people of different ethnic backgrounds. There are also advantages for business and the wider community. By promoting greater fairness, it will encourage employee commitment, reduce staff turnover, and act as a spur to productivity and competitiveness.'

It is acknowledged that criticism exists about the introduction of a NMW, especially in the areas of:

- **pay differentials**
- business costs
- competitiveness
- prices
- employment
- public sector finances

However, the LPC has surveyed the experience of many other countries which have introduced a NMW, and offers the following two conclusions:

'On the **pay differentials** aspect, almost all studies find that a NMW does lead to a compression of the earnings distribution i.e. the pressure to restore **pay differentials** is limited.'

'Sensibly set minimum wages have contributed successfully to social policy without a significant adverse effect on employment?

(a) Define each of the following terms and state how, in each case, it might be affected by the National Minimum Wage (NMW):
   (i) in-work poverty   [2 marks]
   (ii) work incentives   [2 marks]
   (iii) pay differentials.   [2 marks]
(b) Explain why the introduction of 'sensibly set minimum wages' may not have a 'significant adverse effect on employment' (line 26).
                               [4 marks]

(c) Explain why the LPC might believe that the introduction of a NMW should bring 'greater equality in pay between the sexes and between people of different ethnic backgrounds'.

[6 marks]

(d) Discuss the possible effects of the introduction of a NMW both on the distribution of income and on the competitiveness of the British economy. [9 marks]

Chapter Five

Employment and unemployment

'Rising unemployment and recession have been the price we have to pay (or well worth paying) to get inflation down.'
Norman Lamont, Chancellor of the Exchequer 1991

The working population is divided between those people who are in work and those people seeking work i.e. the employed and the unemployed. The total size of the workforce can change as more men and women are encouraged to work or the size of population of working age increases due to rises in the numbers in that age group or through gains from net migration. The **employment rate** measures the total number employed expressed as a percentage of all the people of working age. This percentage has been edging up with additional support to get people back into the workforce and stands at about 75% nationally (the EU average is 64%). However, there are considerable regional variations dependent on the ease of availability of jobs. Generally, the more people in work, the higher the total level of production, the higher the level of income or Gross Domestic Product (GDP) and the higher the standard of living. In this sense, at least, work is good for us.

Employment

Table 5 shows the changes that have occurred in the pattern of

Table 5 Changing employment shares in the UK 1950–2000

% of employees in employment	1950	1960	1970	1980	1990a	2000b
Agriculture, forestry and fishing	5.60	4.10	1.74	1.57	1.37	1.27
Mining, supply of electricity, gas and water	5.16	4.73	3.68	3.19	1.74	0.86
Manufacturing	38.02	37.66	38.69	30.28	20.52	16.52
Transport, storage and communication	8.00	6.97	6.94	6.52	6.07	6.09
Construction	6.66	6.51	5.88	5.37	5.36	4.73
Wholesale and retail distribution	12.74	13.88	12.08	14.61	15.79	17.04
Services	23.82	26.16	30.98	38.47	49.15	53.50

a) Figures for 1990 and 2000 refer to UK, earlier years refer to GB.
b) December 1999.
Sources: Ministry of Labour Gazette, Department of Employment Gazette, Employment Gazette, Labour Market Trends (various years).

employment in the UK from 1950 to 2000.

Over the period there has been a trend of the continued decline of employment in the primary and secondary industries and the growth of the service sector. After the Second World War some of the largest employers were the coal, steel and shipbuilding industries. Today more people are employed in Indian restaurants than in these three industries combined. The service sector now accounts for more than 70% of employment compared with 37% in 1950 while employment in manufacturing has fallen by nearly a half. This process is similar to that experienced by most advanced economies over the same time period and has been referred to as a period of **de-industrialization.**

The trend has not been consistent. Table 6 illustrates the magnitude of the change in each decade.

The most dramatic period of change occurred in the 1970s and 80s with a slow-down in the rate of change in the 1990s. A range of factors helps to explain this emerging picture. In agriculture there have been moves towards larger farms, increased mechanization and improved yields from animals and crops in order to drive down costs. Industrial scale output has been the result but with reduced demand for farm workers. Price controls under the EU's **Common Agriculture Policy** and the market power of the supermarkets have also put the squeeze on farmers. If prices are fixed the only way farmers can increase profit is to drive down costs and the supermarket chains are now prepared to source their purchases globally to put pressure on domestic suppliers. One result of this has been cheap food but an unwelcome consequence has been deteriorating quality, BSE and Foot

Table 6 Change in % employment in each decade 1950–2000

Change in % over decade	1950s	1960s	1970s	1980s	1990s
Agriculture, forestry and fishing	−1.50	−2.35	−0.18	−0.20	−0.1
Mining, supply of electricity, gas and water	−0.44	−1.04	−0.50	−1.44	−0.88
Manufacturing	−0.36	1.03	−8.41	−9.76	−4.00
Transport, storage and communication	−1.03	−0.03	−0.42	−0.45	0.02
Construction	−0.15	−0.62	−0.51	−0.01	−0.64
Wholesale and retail distribution	1.14	−1.80	2.53	1.18	1.25
Services	2.34	4.82	7.48	10.68	4.35

Sources: Ministry of Labour Gazette, Department of Employment Gazette, Employment Gazette, Labour Market Trends (various years).

and Mouth disease. The change in taste towards more labour intensive, organic food is accelerating with each new food scare and is growing in importance.

Developing technology, particularly the application of computer technology, has made a major impact on the numbers of people needed to produce manufactured goods. Efficiency and total production have increased but employment has fallen. Manufacturing is still relatively labour intensive and does still employ over 3 million people. In the last 50 years this industry has witnessed a shift towards global operators ready to locate production plants where unit costs are lowest, mainly in the Far East and Eastern Europe. A loss of relative competitiveness through low productivity and a high exchange rate has pushed production away from the UK and the setting up of the Euro zone has further encouraged companies to shift production out of the UK. Capital is highly mobile. Trans-national companies chase higher profits across the world. The UK has been forced to adjust to this by concentrating on high value-added production making more sophisticated use of the new technology such as bio and environmental technology and pharmaceuticals.

The service industries have boomed. This is one area where the UK does possess **comparative advantage**. The financial sector has a highly respected international reputation for fair dealing; it is highly profitable and has attracted a lot of overseas business. Retail and distribution employment has grown despite the fact that the development of the large supermarket chains has led to the decline of the small shop. The leisure and hospitality industries have grown with the rise in the general level of incomes and e-commerce has expanded rapidly.

Does the shift in employment patterns matter?

The free market answer would be: no. Changes in employment patterns simply reflect responses to the changing signals of the market. If some areas of economic activity become less profitable, resources will move to areas of greater profitability. The nature of the change is immaterial. Competition from other countries will drive down prices, increase choice and increase the efficiency of UK manufacturers although some may be driven out of business. To try to protect inefficient manufacturers would lead to a waste of scarce resources. For years the Multi-Fibre Agreement aimed to keep cheap imported textiles out of the UK market. Jobs were protected in the textile industry but the cost was paid for by the consumer in the form of higher prices. The free market view is that it is more efficient to buy textiles from cheaper producers overseas and for the home manufacturers to concentrate on products where they have some comparative advantage. Free markets theoretically work for the benefit of all.

However, there are employment implications. If a major motor manufacturing company closes down a plant there will be a **multiplier effect** causing other related jobs, often in the same part of the country, to be destroyed. As some sectors of the economy are contracting, some will be expanding and we would expect workers to be moving from one sector to the other. The problem here is that employees often possess employer specific skills and have been used to good wages so they may not find it easy to switch to other occupations in other industries. Workers may be prepared to wait for a longer time in the hope that a similar job emerges in the old industry. New jobs may require new skills, extra training, a geographical move and pay lower wages and so people may find themselves unemployed for long periods of time during the transition stage. Higher unemployment represents its own waste of resources and imposes costs on society such as extra benefit costs, social and domestic costs, the costs of lower tax revenues and the costs of lost production. More recent attempts to raise the level of transferable skills in the workforce recognize this difficulty, aim to increase the employability of workers and reduce the periods people may spend unemployed between jobs.

Implicit in the discussion so far has been the assumption that all free international trade is fair trade. Unfortunately, this is often not the case. Developed countries may make use of hidden subsidies to protect manufacturers or impose hidden forms of protection whereas developing countries may make use of child labour, pay poverty wages and allow terrible working conditions The situation is rarely transparent. Some might argue that it is unfair to expect firms in the UK to compete with the rock bottom cost base of companies in the developing world. In Economics we need to question the causes of the differing cost structures. Low wages may be the result of genuine factors. There may be a large workforce of working age willing to work for relatively low amounts of money. Prohibiting trade of this kind will hold back the process of development and keep prices high in developed countries. The theory of comparative advantage should be allowed to run its course.

Should child labour and inhuman working conditions be tolerated if it leads to cheaper trainers? (See the article on page 60.)

The decline of manufacturing will also affect the UK's performance on its **balance of payments**. The balance of payments records all transactions between the UK and the rest of the world. The UK has regularly made a deficit on its trade in visible goods but this has been

Child labour scandal hits Adidas

BRUTALITY, POOR WAGES AND 15-HOUR DAYS IN THE ASIAN SWEATSHOPS

They are the ultimate status symbols for sports stars and street-conscious young people. With their trademark three stripes, Adidas clothes cost a small fortune to buy and are promoted by world-famous names such as England skipper David Beckham, Olympic heptathlete Denise Lewis and Russian tennis player Anna Kournikova.

But the company will this week become embroiled in controversy when the European Parliament hears of the barbaric treatment of employees in Indonesian sweatshop factories supplying the German conglomerate.

The Parliament will be told that clothes for Adidas were made in two factories using child labour, forced overtime and sexual harassment. Representatives of workers in two Indonesian factories supplying the German company, will tell Euro MPs that in the Nikomax Gemilang and Tuntex factories, in the Indonesian capital of Jakarta, children as young as 15 were:

• made to work 15-hour days;
• expected to do at least 70 hours a week and punished for refusing to do overtime;
• paid less than $60 a month, rates below the International Labour Organization's demand for a living wage;
• penalized for taking leave during medical difficulties and had illegal deductions taken from wages as punishments for minor misdemeanours.

Sports goods companies have been criticised for exploiting workers in the developing world before. There was a storm just before the 1998 World Cup, after footballs bearing the Manchester United club crest were being made by child labourers in India, working for as little as 6p an hour. Cricket Ball manufacturers were also criticized.

A report by Christian Aid revealed that children, some as young as seven, were regularly used in the production of a wide range of sports goods in India. Most of the £13 million worth of goods went to Britain.

Last year a worker from a Bangkok factory for Adidas claimed that for less than £1 per day she worked 12-hour shifts, producing sportswear, shoes and replica kits for the company.

She claimed conditions were poor in the Thai factory and the management acted brutally to meet large orders within a limited time, often denying workers statutory rights such as holidays and sick pay. The accusations are similar to those made by the Indonesian workers.

The woman was eventually sacked in 1998 along with 23 others after they formed a union in an attempt to win more rights. The factory management claimed she was a disruptive influence.

Most Adidas goods are produced in Third World countries, particularly Asia, with orders awarded to locally run factories. Many orders are sub-contracted at local level, leading to claims that the companies have little idea of where and how their goods are produced.

Adidas denies ignoring workers' rights for the sake of profit, claiming they have strict labour codes and constantly monitoring wage levels and conditions to ensure a good worker environment.

Jason Burke, *The Observer,* 19 November 2000

assisted by a good performance on 'invisible items': the trade in services where the UK generally makes a surplus. Further growth in the deficit on the trading balance will mean that there is an even bigger gap to be made up with other transactions. Money can be borrowed for a certain time to make up this gap but a continuous borrowing requirement could restrict the UK's ability to borrow in the future and this could take away some of the UK's freedom of manoeuvre. A lender of money to the UK could attach conditions to the loan. Being part of the Single European Market should reduce this problem since the UK is, in effect, one part of the larger market. There is less need to worry about the trade performance of one part of the market just as we do not worry too much about whether the North East or the Midlands are running a trade deficit with the rest of the UK.

Economies may respond sluggishly to change and this is one of the main causes of the economic problems associated with unemployment. In the absence of the free market assumption of perfect mobility of factors of production, governments must decide whether to intervene in order to protect jobs at the cost of higher prices or accept a higher level of unemployment in the search for economic efficiency.

Unemployment

The measurement of unemployment

Unemployment is an economic concern. It is one of the main macro-economic challenges faced by governments. It represents an under-utilized resource which is not contributing to the output and welfare of the economy. The government publishes information on the numbers of unemployed in two ways. The unemployed may be entitled to receive jobseekers' allowance and a record is taken of the numbers claiming this benefit. Hence this method of measurement is known as the **Claimant Count**. It is a snap shot of unemployment but does not include those people who may be looking for work but are not entitled to benefit. The government can manipulate the figure by changing the rules which govern who can claim benefit and there are also those who might describe themselves as not in the labour force but who might, nevertheless, move into work if the right opportunity comes along. The **International Labour Organization (ILO)** measures unemployment by surveying people and asking them whether they regard themselves as employed or unemployed. This measure includes benefit claimants and others and can be used more easily for international comparison.

It is clear that over the last century there have been periods of varying levels of unemployment. Extreme unemployment was experienced

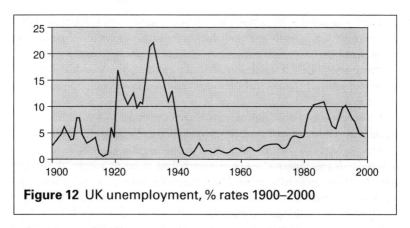

Figure 12 UK unemployment, % rates 1900–2000

between the two World Wars, low unemployment from 1940 through to the late 1970s and rising unemployment until the late 1990s. As economists we need to be able to explain why these trends occurred and to see whether this knowledge gives us a mechanism for predicting future unemployment.

The causes of unemployment

Within the long-term trends in unemployment shown in Table 7 there appear to be rather shorter fluctuations or cycles when unemployment rises but then falls back. These cyclical periods last for about 5 to 10 years and describe what is happening to the economy as it moves through periods of fast growth, slows down into recession then into recovery before growth rates start rising again or, as some politicians would put it, from boom to bust. Similar patterns are experienced by other economies which suggest that there are forces at work to create such cycles within economic systems.

A range of theories attempt to explain the existence of these **business or economic cycles**. Investment undertaken by businesses takes place in bursts as the key decision-makers are influenced by future expectations. If they believe the economy is about to experience a period of rising sales then they will commit more funds to investment or bring forward growth plans. These decisions generate more investment from other firms and a multiplier effect is created on investment and jobs. During the early stages of the cycle, as consumption rises, there may be an **accelerator** at work pushing firms to invest at a faster rate. However, at some point the pace of investment slows, expectations take a dive and the rate of new investment falls away. It is this process that then forces the economy into recession and unemployment rises.

Economic cycles have also been linked to the political cycle when governments tend to engineer boom periods prior to a general election to generate a feel-good factor which can translate into votes. After the election the government may need to cut back on spending or raise taxes which will choke off demand and push the economy towards recession.

Economies are now heavily inter-dependent. Growth or recession phases experienced by the UK's trading partners will quickly transfer to the domestic economy: a boom in the USA brings rising demand for UK goods and services so the UK also benefits, a recession in Europe or Japan reduces the demand for UK products and drags the UK economy into recession.

Over the much longer term changes in technology bring their cyclical effects. At the beginning of the twenty-first century the world is witnessing an Internet and information technology revolution that may alter the way economies operate in ways difficult to predict. It is likely that during the development stage of this technological shift huge expansion opportunities will occur, the dot com companies will mushroom and jobs should be generated. At some point the speed of change will slow as the technological cycle reaches maturity and moves into decline and higher levels of unemployment may be felt across the world. One idea expressed by Kondratieff, is that such technological cycles take anything up to 50 years to work themselves out and might explain the high unemployment of the 1930s and the 1980s.

J. M. Keynes attributed the high unemployment of the Depression years of the 1930s to a lack of aggregate or total demand in the economy. The economic orthodoxy at the time suggested that there was little that governments could do to alleviate the problem but Keynes's intervention gave a possible way out: if governments could boost aggregate demand by increasing their own spending at times of high unemployment, then consumption would rise and employment increase. This broad approach was adopted by governments after 1945 and heralded a sustained period of low unemployment.

Another explanation of long-term unemployment is the structural change that occurs in an economy through the process of deindustrialization. As economies adapt to the change some people will be unemployed when industries are contracting and before alternative jobs have been created. This **structural unemployment** can be of particular importance in certain parts of the country suffering from major industrial closures and is reflected in the wide variation of unemployment rates shown in Tables 8a and 8b.

Table 8a Regional unemployment

ILO unemployment rates

Percentages, Spring each year, not seasonally adjusted

	1992	1993	1994	1995	1996	1997	1998	1999
United Kingdom	9.7	10.3	9.6	8.6	8.2	7.1	6.1	6.0
North East	11.9	12.0	12.5	11.4	10.8	9.8	8.2	10.1
North West &								
Merseyside	10.1	10.8	10.3	9.0	8.4	6.9	6.6	6.2
North West	9.2	9.8	9.6	8.3	7.3	6.3	5.6	5.5
Merseyside	14.0	15.3	13.5	11.7	13.3	9.6	10.9	9.6
Yorkshire and Humber	10.1	10.0	9.9	8.7	8.1	8.1	7.0	6.6
East Midlands	8.8	9.1	8.3	7.5	7.4	6.3	4.9	5.2
West Midlands	10.7	11.8	10.0	9.0	9.2	6.8	6.3	6.8
Eastern	7.7	9.2	8.2	7.5	6.2	5.9	5.0	4.2
London	12.0	13.2	13.1	11.5	11.3	9.1	8.1	7.5
South East	7.8	8.0	7.1	6.4	6.0	5.2	4.3	3.6
South West	9.1	9.2	7.5	7.8	6.3	5.2	4.5	4.7
England	9.7	10.3	9.5	8.6	8.1	6.9	6.0	5.8
Wales	8.9	9.6	9.3	8.8	8.3	8.4	6.7	7.1
Scotland	9.5	10.2	10.0	8.3	8.7	8.5	7.4	7.4
Northern Ireland	12.3	12.5	11.7	11.0	9.7	7.5	7.3	7.2

Sources: *Labour Force Survey*, Office for National Statistics: Department of
Economic Development, Northern Ireland

    The regional figures on unemployment do arouse concern because
they indicate the kind of prosperity gap which exists between the North
and South parts of the UK and that little seems to have affected this
divide over the years. Try drawing up a league table going from the
region with the lowest unemployment to the area with the highest to
see if there has been any change in the order over the years. It is difficult
to shape economic policy to meet the needs of all of the regions. High
interest rates may be introduced to control house prices and inflation in
the South East when other parts of the UK suffer no such problems. The
regional figures themselves can be misleading because within each
region there are wide variations in prosperity. In the North West, for
example, Knowsley in Liverpool suffers from an unemployment rate of
more than twice the average and Ribble Valley one-fifth of the average.

Table 8b Regional unemployment

Claimant count rates[1,2]
Analysis by Government Office Regions[3]

	Percentages, seasonally adjusted						
	1992	1993	1994	1995	1996	1997	1998
Annual averages							
United Kingdom	9.7	10.3	9.3	8.0	7.3	5.5	4.7
North East	12.1	12.9	12.4	11.3	10.3	8.4	7.5
North West	10.5	10.6	9.9	8.5	7.8	6.1	5.3
Yorkshire and Humber	9.9	10.2	9.6	8.6	7.9	6.3	5.5
East Midlands	9.0	9.5	8.7	7.4	6.7	4.9	4.0
West Midlands	10.3	10.8	9.9	8.1	7.2	5.5	4.7
Eastern	8.7	9.4	8.1	6.6	5.9	4.1	3.3
London	10.5	11.6	10.7	9.4	8.6	6.4	5.3
South Eastern	8.0	8.8	7.3	5.9	5.1	3.4	2.7
South West	9.2	9.5	8.1	6.8	6.1	4.3	3.5
Wales	10.0	10.3	9.3	8.5	8.0	6.4	5.6
Scotland	9.4	9.7	9.3	7.9	7.7	6.4	5.7
Northern Ireland	13.8	13.7	12.6	11.2	10.8	8.1	7.4

[1] The number of unemployment-related benefit claimants as a percentage of the estimated total workforce (the sum of claimants, employee jobs self-employed, participants on work related government training programmes and HM Forces) at mid-year.
[2] Seasonally adjusted and excluding claimants under 18, consistent with current coverage.
[3] New geographical boundaries were introduced in May 1997 for UK regions.
Source: *Labour Market Statistics,* Office for National Statistics

Another indicator of structural unemployment is the length of time people remain unemployed. Areas that have suffered industrial closures, with few alternative employment opportunities, are likely to have more long-term unemployed. This group can lose touch with the job market, lose skills and can become discouraged. In areas with a more diverse range of employers unemployment will be a much more short-term problem.

The European Union does recognize that the development of the Single European Market could leave some parts of the EU disadvantaged and, consequently, it has developed a **regional policy** which directs funds to the poorest areas. The EU has set up four structural funds: The European Regional Development Fund (ERDF), The European Social Fund (ESF), The European Agricultural Guidance and Guarantee Fund (EAGGF) and the Financial Instrument for Fisheries Guidance (FIFG). Regions may be classified in one of three categories for support: Objective 1 directed at the poorest parts of the EU and including Merseyside, South Wales and the Valleys, South Yorkshire and Cornwall; Objective 2 providing specific help to areas facing particular structural problems; Objective 3 providing money to assist schemes to support the improvement of education, training and employment. Over the period 2000–06 the EU structural finds will spend Euro 213 billion on support, nearly a third of the total EU regional budget. Areas receiving support develop their own plans to generate higher income job opportunities in the local area and build greater prosperity for the future. There are criticisms of the way these funds are put in place. They aim to achieve a range of political, economic, social and environmental objectives which may not all be compatible at the same time, the effectiveness is open to question: for example Merseyside received the support for six years but because of lack of success returned for another round of support in the next phase. There are concerns about the identification process of areas qualifying for support and the monitoring and evaluation systems.

A lack of flexibility in the labour market could be seen to be a major cause of unemployment. If the labour market operates as a free market, there should be no unemployment. Whenever there is a surplus of labour, wage levels should fall and the demand for labour increase. Therefore, if ever there is unemployment it must be the result of wages not moving to their equilibrium level and this wage 'stickiness' could be caused by the actions of trade unions, government action on minimum wages or benefits or employers paying over the odds to attract workers to them. Such unemployment is known as **disequilibrium unemployment** and is a form of labour market failure.

Unemployment may occur because of a **mismatch** between the supply of labour and the demand for it. Labour may be available but it may not have the right skills or be in the right place for the vacancies which exist. Some of this **frictional unemployment** will be relatively short-term and is due to the imperfect mobility of resources. Additionally, unemployment can occur because of a lack of appropriate information, people simply not being aware of the job opportunities available. Some parts of the country such as Blackpool and the Isle of Wight experience **seasonal unemployment** due to the seasonal nature of employment in tourism. Plenty of workers are needed at certain times of the year but not at others. Each month there is a flow of up to 300,000 people moving into and out of employment and this movement and the short periods of unemployment are a normal part of the economic process. During our working lives we can expect to change our jobs from seven to ten times.

The 'natural' or equilibrium rate of unemployment

Since economies are always undergoing industrial change to a greater or lesser extent, it is unrealistic to expect unemployment to be zero. There will always be friction within the system creating some unemployment. Therefore, it could be said that there is a certain **'natural' rate of unemployment** when the labour market is in equilibrium. What that level is depends on the way institutions work in the economy. If there are powerful institutions such as trade unions which prevent wage levels from reflecting free market forces, the 'natural' rate of unemployment may be high. As the market is freed up from institutional constraints the 'natural' rate will fall. If people are not prepared to take the jobs on offer at the wages offered then they could be regarded as being **voluntarily unemployed**. The idea of a 'natural' rate is appealing to those believing that there should be less intervention in the economy. A 'natural' rate suggests that a government should not attempt to reduce unemployment below a certain level because it will only lead to more inflation and a higher level of unemployment for the future. The level of unemployment consistent with low inflation may be referred to as the Non-accelerating inflation rate of unemployment (**NAIRU**): Un in Fig 13 where PP1 represents the Phillips curve showing a trade-off between inflation and the rate of unemployment. The policy implication of this is that if the Government tries to boost aggregate demand to get unemployment below Un then the result will be higher inflation (in Figure 13 there is a movement from point Un to point a). As wages rise the unemployed may be attracted into jobs believing that they will be better off than previously – they suffer from **money illusion**. However, as they realize that prices have also risen and that they are no better off in real terms, they drop out of the workforce again shown by a movement from point a to point b and the economy is left with higher inflation at level X and the same high level of unemployment. Further attempts to reduce unemployment by boosting aggregate demand lead to even higher levels of inflation and have no long-term effect on the level of unemployment which sticks at Un. Un appears to be the level of unemployment consistent with low inflation or NAIRU. Un might also be described as the 'natural' rate of unemployment since it cannot be reduced below the level Un.

There are questions about the idea of a 'natural' rate of unemployment. It is difficult to locate the position of the rate with any precision and it can change over time. If the 'natural' rate is deemed to be at, say, 2 million then there is an acceptance of a considerable waste of resources and all the problems that flow from high unemployment.

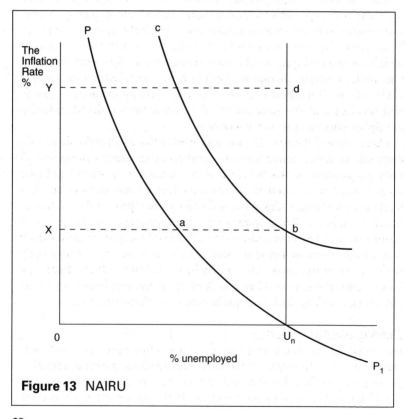

Figure 13 NAIRU

Critics argue that the whole idea is there to justify government inaction. But it is also clear that any positive government intervention is not cost-free and there will be different views about how effectively the money can be targeted. Expenditure on government schemes such as **New Deal** aimed at reducing unemployment can be brought into question if there is evidence that any extra employment might have been created anyway through the normal growth in the economy.

The costs of unemployment

Apart from the general waste of economic resources, why else should we be concerned about the numbers of people unemployed?

There is a financial cost to the taxpayer in that the jobseekers' allowance is paid for out of general taxation and, whilst people are on benefit, they are paying fewer taxes on their income and their expenditure. So, government expenditure increases while revenue falls. There may also be a need to spend government money on special schemes to create employment. This raises issues of opportunity cost since it is always possible to think of many other beneficial programmes such as hospitals, pensions and schools on which the money could have been spent. The largest cost is likely to be the cost of the lost output which the unemployed would have produced had they been in work. One million people unemployed might have produced approximately $1/25^{th}$ of the GDP of the country or about £20 billion worth of goods and services and the production of this output would have had a multiplier effect on the wider economy.

There are social costs. The unemployed suffer from more ill-health, domestic violence, crime and suicide than other groups in society. A cycle of poverty occurs where children growing up in unemployed households fair less well at school, have fewer opportunities, are less likely to enter higher education and end up unemployed themselves or in low paid, low skilled employment. Unemployment does not affect all groups in society to the same extent. Some ethnic groups suffer from much higher unemployment rates than others and so consequently suffer more of the costs. This might be to do with cultural factors, a lack of entrepreneurial skills, a lack of opportunities in certain inner-city areas, a lack of skills and qualifications or discrimination.

Solving unemployment

It is possible to reduce unemployment but it is first necessary to identify the cause of that unemployment. Governments have **monetary, fiscal or direct policy** at their disposal and can use them to counter the causes of the different types of unemployment. If the government chooses to make use of **Keynesian policies** it will be able to adopt a counter-cyclical strategy to try to smooth out the worst effects of the business cycle. If a recession is caused by a lack of aggregate demand then the government can boost demand by either increasing its own spending or by cutting taxes. The Republican Bush administration in the USA placed tax cutting as one of its major priorities. At a time when the economy appeared to be heading towards recession, even the Democrats could see some merit in this good Keynesian approach although they might well disagree with who should be the main recipients of the tax cuts. The Japanese launched massive spending programmes to get them out of recession in the late 1990s.

Adjustment of interest rates also helps the cause. A cut in rates is likely to lead to a rise in borrowing which will stimulate demand and act to prevent recession. In the UK, the Monetary Policy Committee of the Bank of England now has control of interest rates but it does monitor the progress of the economy and responds to either recessionary or inflationary pressures by changing the Bank's Base Rate. Potentially the government could intervene if it was dissatisfied with the Bank's performance and take back monetary control directly although there might well be a cost in terms of the loss of financial trust from the City of London financial institutions which could lead onto other adverse repercussions.

A freeing up of the labour market can solve the problem of disequilibrium unemployment. If there are constraints that are holding wages above their equilibrium level then the obvious response is to remove those constraints. In the past legislation to limit the power of trade unions and policies to privatize industry to create much more local pay bargaining has helped to break up the labour market and reduce the potential disruption of strike action. The National Minimum Wage could be said to impede the operation of a free market but much depends on where the wage level is set. The USA does have minimum wage rates but these are set so low that they have little effect on the labour market.

Structural unemployment could be countered by an active regional policy designed to make the regions attractive to inward investment. A set of nine English Regional Development Agencies, the Scottish Parliament, the Welsh Assembly and the Northern Ireland Executive control much of the funding which goes to the regions. These bodies are better equipped to identify local priorities and so get better value for money from government expenditure. These bodies are directly charged with the responsibility to promote employment and to further economic development and regeneration. The alternative to the interventionist approach would be to wait until the price differentials between the regions becomes so great that companies eventually decide to move production to take advantage of lower costs. The problem here is that this process takes a long time and, once established, firms are reluctant to move. Governments could sit back and watch the wealth divide grow wider but most choose to implement some policies directed at evening out income and wealth distribution. This is developed in more detail in Chapter 6.

An alternative approach would be to encourage the unemployed to move from the poorer areas to the richer but this could have serious negative economic effects. De-population from some parts of the country leaves the social capital such as hospitals and schools under-utilized while the prosperous areas begin to suffer from the effects of over-crowding including congestion, pollution and soaring house prices and wages. As people desert an area more jobs go from that area as demand falls. Long-term prosperity is better achieved by a balanced growth across the country.

To protect jobs in manufacturing, a stable economic environment seems essential with low interest rates, low taxation rates and a competitive exchange rate. Whether these conditions are likely to be achieved by entry into the Single European Currency is open to debate but for companies selling into the European market there do seem to be benefits from dealing in one, rather than fifteen, currencies. The final decision about entry will be as much about politics and, probably, prejudice as it is about economics. Certainly, a strong case is made out by the pro-euro camp to suggest that jobs will be lost if the UK does not join (see the article on page 72).

The problem of a mismatch between the type of labour demanded and the type of labour supplied can be improved with the provision of better information, measures to assist mobility and training. **Supply-side policies** which try to improve the productivity of the workforce and increase employability will help firms to expand with fewer recruitment difficulties and will help the unemployed to find jobs. Just as there is a responsibility on the unemployed to update skills to be ready for job opportunities as they arise, there is also a responsibility on the firm to invest in its workforce by providing appropriate training. Small firms often struggle to provide training and here there is a role for the government to plug this gap.

Seasonal unemployment is of short duration. Some hotels and tourist facilities attempt to extend their season or encourage workers to be trained in a range of skills which could provide work all year round.

In discussing the strategies to counter unemployment it is possible to forget the human tragedy that unemployment causes. If a factory closes

40,000 jobs 'lost by failure to join euro'

MPs FEAR ELECTION BACKLASH OVER MANUFACTURING CRISIS

BY GABY HINSLIFF CHIEF POLITICAL CORRESPONDENT

Britain's failure to join the euro may have cost up to 40,000 manufacturing jobs this year, according to powerful new evidence facing the Government.

The analysis, following last week's announcement of redundancies at the Vauxhall car plant, will fuel fresh demands from backbenchers for action to save traditional industries.

The Amalgamated Engineering and Electrical Union leader, Sir Ken Jackson, who has warned that the future for car manufacturing is 'virtually nil' if Britain stays outside the euro, lashed out yesterday at Eurosceptics, accusing them of making it virtually impossible for the Government to reassure nervous investors.

The Britain in Europe figures suggest that in the past five weeks alone more than 4,900 jobs have gone, due at least in part to currency volatility – inability to cope with a strong pound and a weak euro – nearly half of them at Vauxhall, whose strongly pro-euro chief executive Nick Reilly has worked closely with BiE and admitted the strength of the pound 'has not helped' in the decision to downgrade its Luton plant.

Others across the country range from the 100 jobs lost at Eliza Tinsley in Coventry – whose chief executive said that 'currencies are working against us and we have to cut costs' – to 1,200 jobs at the textile manufacturers Coats Viyella, who cited 'the strong pound and cheap foreign competition'. Between January and November, up to 35,000 jobs went across the country in similar circumstances.

Meanwhile, Nissan's flagship plant in Sunderland is at risk if the parent company decides next month to build the new Micra in France, within the euro zone.

The closures will spark passionate debate over whether the euro issue is to blame, or market forces squeezing older industries. Although the strong pound has been cited at least as a factor in all the cases listed by BiE, critics argue it is not the only cause.

The euro won't necessarily make everything rosy because there are round about 20 million cars produced in Europe and only about 16 million buyers,' said Fraser Kemp, Labour's former election organizer and the MP for Houghton and Washington, which includes many Nissan workers.

'But the euro does have a particular impact on manufacturing because the investment required and the decision-making process is over such a timescale that what you really want is stability.'

The Observer, 17 December 2000

down with the loss of 700 jobs it will be headline news for a few days. This means that 700 families are affected, or up to 2800 people. In addition more local jobs will disappear as the negative multiplier kicks in. Suppliers will be affected as well as local shops and services. Possibly three jobs are lost for every one in the original firm or up to 2100 affecting another group of families. As people move away from the area, more jobs go. Local areas can be devastated unless a major support programme is launched. It is the human cost of unemployment which can be the most serious.

The picture is not all gloom. In fact there has been considerable success in reducing unemployment and the rates being seen today are the lowest in 25 years. Figures of less than one million contrast starkly with the record during the 1980s and 90s. It would seem that governments can make an impact on unemployment and leaving it totally to the labour market need not be the only option. Perhaps the last few years indicate that we can have low inflation **and** low unemployment and not, as Norman Lamont suggested, one at the expense of the other.

KEY WORDS

Employment rate	Structural unemployment
Deindustrialization	Regional policy
Common Agricultural Policy (CAP)	Disequilibrium unemployment
	Mismatch
Comparative advantage	Frictional unemployment
Multiplier effect	Seasonal unemployment
Balance of payments	'Natural' rate of unemployment
Invisible items	Voluntary unemployment
Claimant Count	NAIRU
International Labour Organization (ILO)	Money illusion
	New Deal
Business/economic cycles	Monetary/fiscal/direct policy
Accelerator	Keynesian policies
Supply-side policies	

Useful websites

An international forum for Regional Development policy and research
   www.regional-studies-assoc.ac.uk
Government New Deal site www.newdeal.gov.uk
Government Employment Service site – Bacon and Eltis 'Too few producers' www.employmentservice.gov.uk
Extracts from J. K. Galbraith essay, *Time to ditch the NAIRU*
   www.vcn.bc.ca/timework/nairu.htm

Site of the Federal Reserve Bank of San Francisco www.frbsf.org
Discussion of the 'natural' rate from New York University
www.equity.stern.nyu.edu

Further reading
Bamford, C., and Grant, S., Chapter 6 in *The UK Economy in a Global Context*, Heinemann Educational, 2000.

Grant, S., and Vidler, C., Part 2 Unit 17 in *Economics in Context*, Heinemann, 2000.

Griffiths, A., and Wall, S., (eds), Chapter 23 in *Applied Economics*, 8th edn, Longman, 1999.

Smith, D., Chapter 6 in *UK Current Economic Policy*, 2nd edn, Heinemann Educational, 1999.

Essay topics
1. (a) Examine the economic costs of unemployment to society.
   [40 marks]
   (b) Compare employment subsidies and reduced unemployment benefits as methods of reducing unemployment. [60 marks]
   Source: Edexcel, Q5, Paper 2, January 1998.
2. (a) Explain how unemployment can be caused by labour market failures at the micro-economic level. [8 marks]
   (b) Discuss the extent to which unemployment can be caused by demand management policies at the macro-economic level.
   [12 marks]
   Source: OCR, Q3, Paper 4387, November 2000.

Data response question
Edexcel, Q2, Paper 3A, June 1999

Examine Figures 1–6 which relate to the UK labour market.

Figure 1 Percentage of UK employees affected by the National Minimum Wage, by industry

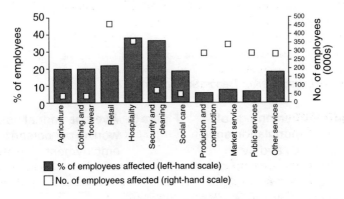

Figure 2 Characteristics of the lowest paid, UK, 1997

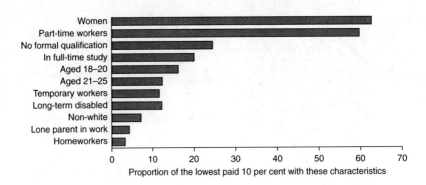

(Source: Report of the Low Pay Commission, June 1998 © Crown Copyright 1998)

Figure 3 Percentage of employees who were temporary: UK, spring 1996; not seasonally adjusted

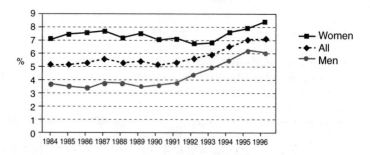

(Source: *Labour Market Trends*, September 1997)

Figure 4 Percentage of population aged 65 and over

Figure 5 Average annual hours worked per person in employment

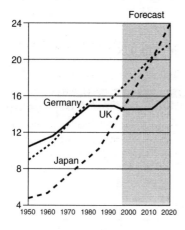

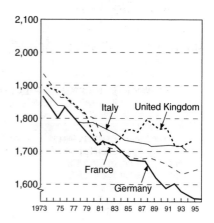

(Source: *The Independent*, 17 February, 1998)

(Source: *OECD*, 17 June, 1997)

Figure 6 Hours worked by full-time employees and self-employed, UK, weekly, winter 1997–98

	Men	Women	All
People without a second job (OOOs)	13,092	6,330	19,422
Average weekly hours worked	39.0	33.7	37.2
People with a second job (OOOs) Average	414	240	654
weekly hours worked in both jobs	48.8	42.2	46.4

Notes (i) Data based on respondents' own estimates, not actual hours worked.

(ii) Data includes paid and unpaid overtime but excludes meal breaks.

(Source: *Labour Market Trends*, August 1998.)

(a) How might the incidence of low pay in different industries shown in Figure 1 be explained, using the information in Figure 2?

[8 marks]

(b) With reference to Figure 3, identify the factors which might explain the trend in:

(i) the use of temporary workers by employers;

(ii) the willingness of employees to accept temporary work.

[6 marks]

(c) Examine the economic implications of the trends shown in Figure 4 for both employers and the governments in these three countries.

[7 marks]

(d) With reference to Figures 5 and 6, outline the likely economic effects on individual employees and employers of the UK complying with the EU directive of a maximum 48 hour working week. [4 marks]

Chapter Six

The distribution of income and wealth

'Women constitute half of the world's population, perform nearly two-thirds of its work hours, receive one-tenth of the world's income and own less than one-hundredth of the world's property.'
UN report, 1980

Income is created through the process of transforming raw resources into finished goods and services and selling them at a price. It is the value added at each stage of production that becomes the income of one group or another. Any surplus income can be saved and is accumulated as wealth. One consequence of the way in which labour markets work is that people receive different levels of income and accumulate different levels of wealth. Wide disparity can be considered as a form of market failure. **Income** is a **flow** of earnings received for the services of a particular factor of production over time. In the case of labour, the employee sells labour in return for wages or salaries, the return received by the owners of land is rent, owners of capital receive interest and people using enterprise to create a business earn profits. Wealth represents the value of a **stock** of assets at a certain point in time. So for an individual, income may be the wage earned for the job of a teacher or police officer and wealth is the value of assets held in the form of a bank account, a car and a house.

The income and wealth a person has reflects their ability to buy goods and services produced by the scarce resources of the country. If we think of the total production of goods and services in the UK as a pie, then the more income and wealth a person has, the bigger the slice of the pie they can control. Most of us have tiny or miniscule slices of pie but some people can grow fat on huge chunks. In a market system the people with the highest income and wealth can dictate to a much greater extent, how the resources of the country are to be used. The willingness and ability of people to pay for items determines whether or not those items will be produced. If a few rich citizens want to spend obscene amounts of money on expensive sports cars and luxury yachts then it is likely that a company will be willing to use resources to supply these products. The system has nothing to do with need and nothing to do with fairness.

The distribution of income

Table 9 shows the distribution of income of each of five groups of households from the poorest to the richest. Each quintile group includes 20% of households and the figures record average incomes before any deductions or the addition of benefits. The data shows that the top fifth of households gain over 17 times the income of those in the lowest group but we must remember that the figures are averages and so disguise wide variations within each group. The top fifth with an average income of over £51,000 include some of the seriously high paid members of society and so the gap between high and low income receivers would look far worse if we were comparing the top and bottom 10% or 5%.

Table 9 Average income per household

United Kingdom						£ per year
			Quintile group of households			
	Bottom fifth	Next fifth	Middle fifth	Next fifth	Top fifth	All house-holds
Average per household						
Wages and Salaries	1,820	5,100	12,490	21,380	38,830	15,930
Imputed income from benefits in kind	10	20	140	310	1,010	300
Self-employment income	410	690	1,380	1,830	5,540	1,970
Occupational pensions, annuities	370	990	1,700	2,010	2,820	1,580
Investment income	230	340	600	920	2,800	980
Other income	100	120	250	240	220	190
Total original income	2,940	7,260	16,570	26,700	51,220	20,940

Source: *Social Trends* 2001

An alternative way to express the income distribution is to look at the percentage of total income each quintile receives. If there was a perfectly even distribution of income then we would expect to see each 20% of the income earners receiving 20% of the total income and this could be shown on a diagram in Figure 14 as a 45-degree line. The actual distribution of income veers away from the straight line and records the Lorenz curve. The greater the gap between the **Lorenz curve** and the diagonal the greater is the inequality in the distribution.

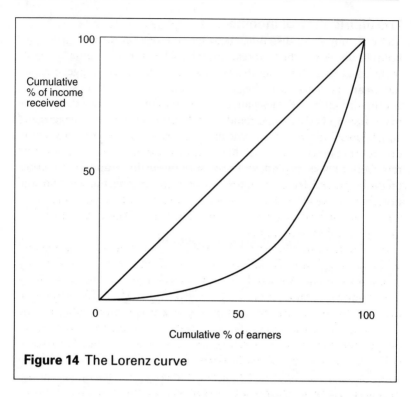

Figure 14 The Lorenz curve

Reports from the Organization for Economic Co-operation and Development (OECD) indicate that during the 1980s and 1990s, inequality increased in many countries but particularly in the UK and USA. This decline in equality offset the trend over the previous 30 years. The reasons for this could be the rising levels of unemployment over that period with an increased number of no-earner households, the large number of people stuck in low paid jobs due to lack of skills and the transitional problems as economies move from being planned to becoming more free market in outlook.

Within the UK income is not spread evenly geographically. In broad terms there still does appear to be a North-South divide, however, it is not as straightforward as it once was. It is the case that the top ten counties with the highest incomes are all in London and the South East but the poorest county is Cornwall and, of the ten most deprived areas, nine are in the North. But within counties there can be considerable variation. Merseyside is one of the poorest areas but it does include Heswell on the Wirral which is one of the country's richest neighbourhoods. Even if income levels do vary greatly this is not the same as comparing living standards and **quality of life**. When the costs of living, particularly housing and transport costs, are taken into account a different picture emerges and the net loss of 50,000 people from London each year suggests that a lot of people do not find living in the capital a dream existence.

Is there a perfect distribution of income which maximizes the welfare of a country? Is there a perfect Lorenz curve? Can we say that a more equal distribution of income is preferable to a more unequal distribution? Here we enter the realms of normative economics. It is relatively easy to explain the causes of inequality and what policies might be pursued to even out the distribution but to say whether one distribution is better than another is more open to value judgments about the qualitative impact of such strategies. The choice becomes more political than economic.

All people want a better rather than a poorer standard of living and so there is a desire to see greater total output in the country and economic growth. All people would also wish to share in those rising living standards and the mark of a civilized society could be found in the way it treats its poor. But there are questions about how governments can best assist the process of income creation. If they tax people and firms too heavily and are too generous with benefits, it could be argued that this will destroy the incentive to work hard and show enterprise. High-income earners may move abroad, businesses may seek friendlier tax regimes elsewhere and investment could flow out of the country. Tax avoidance and tax evasion become a growth industry and the hidden economy thrives. In the long run this could reduce the level of income creation and damage living standards.

However, if the government severely restricts its role then the distribution of income will become more uneven with some groups experiencing dire poverty. Living standards for the fortunate few may improve dramatically but others may lose out. The greater incentives may generate more economic activity as businesses relocate to take advantage of the low tax rates. The degree of inequality is dependent on how successfully the economy takes off and how effectively the 'trickle down' theory operates. Will higher incomes at the top lead to more employment and more benefactors supporting people at the bottom and, even if this is the result, is this the right way to tackle poverty?

Table 10 shows the UK Government's approach indicating the effects of taxes and benefits on the final income of different income quintiles.

Table 10 The redistribution of income through taxes and benefits 1998–99

	Bottom fifth	Next fifth	Middle fifth	Next fifth	Top fifth	All house-holds
Total original income	2,940	7,260	16,570	26,700	51,220	20,940
plus Benefits in cash						
Contributory	2,160	2,690	1,810	1,130	700	1,700
Non-contributory	2,640	2,490	1,640	900	420	1,620
Gross income	7,740	12,430	20,010	28,720	52,340	24,250
less Income tax and NIC	410	1,130	2,950	5,300	11,680	4,290
less Local taxes (net)	500	580	740	840	980	730
Disposable income	6,830	10,730	16,330	22,590	39,680	19,230
less Indirect taxes	2,190	2,650	3,820	4,840	6,340	3,970
Post-tax income	4,630	8,070	12,500	17,750	33,340	15,260
plus Benefits in kind						
Education	1,880	1,200	1,330	980	640	1,210
National Health Service	2,110	2,050	1,910	1,560	1,350	1,800
Housing subsidy	70	60	30	20	–	40
Travel subsidies	40	50	50	60	100	60
School meals and welfare milk	80	30	10	–	–	20
Final income	8,820	11,470	15,840	20,380	35,440	18,390

Source: Office for National Statistics

The table shows that the bottom fifth gain greatly from contributory benefits such as jobseekers' allowance and non-contributory benefits such as child benefit and the State old age pension. People in the top fifth appear to lose most from the payment of income tax and employees' National Insurance Contributions. The overall effect of the redistribution is that the incomes of the top fifth, after tax and benefits have been taken into account, are now only four times higher than the incomes of the lowest fifth. The distribution of income is now far more even.

Redistribution policies

If governments seek a more equal income distribution they largely rely on fiscal policy. Direct taxes such as income tax can be adjusted so that those on higher incomes pay proportionately more than people on low incomes. One of Adam Smith's original principles of taxation included equity or fairness but it is less clear what exactly this means. To illustrate, consider which of the following taxes is fair: a) a tax where each person pays exactly the same amount in tax; b) a tax where each person pays the same percentage of their income in tax; c) a tax where high income earners pay a much higher percentage of their income in tax than low income earners; or d) a tax where high income earners pay a much lower percentage of their income in tax. The UK system includes examples of all four of these kinds of taxes.

Individual taxes may be either more or less progressive. Currently income tax rates vary from 0% on the first tranche of income to a top rate of 40%. This tax has become substantially less redistributive over the years with the top rate coming down from a high of 83% in 1979.

Indirect taxes on expenditure such as VAT or tobacco duties could be made more progressive if more expensive items were taxed at higher rates but generally the government has chosen to go for the simpler option of standard rates on most goods. In Table 10 although the top quintile of income earners do pay more in total in indirect tax, they only pay three times as much as the poorest quintile. With income tax, the top group pays over 28 times the tax compared to the bottom group.

Local taxes such as Council tax are based on property values and could contribute effectively to redistribution but they appear not to as the banding structure used on houses does not relate to the income levels of the owners.

Governments use public expenditure and the benefits system to redistribute income. Benefits are paid at flat rates as **transfer payments** to all who qualify, such as child benefit paid for each child, or are means tested where the level of benefit received is dependent on the level of income of the recipient. The latter is the case for a new children's tax credit where parents with an income up to about £30,000 will be able to claim back over £400 for one child but this is phased out as incomes rise above £40,000. Each kind of benefit has its merits. **Flat rate benefits** achieve 100% take up but go to everybody whether they need them or not. **Means tested benefits** get to the people who really need them but many are put off by the procedure and fail to take up the benefit.

For many people life beyond retirement age would be extremely bleak without the state old-age pension although there is always debate about the level of pension paid. Jobseekers' allowance provides a way of surviving for the unemployed and many of the people in the bottom income quintile are dependent on benefits.

Some benefits, particularly education and health care, are provided free at the point of delivery and these give major support to low-income groups. At present good education and health care are regarded as a right for all although some, mainly higher income, people may choose to opt out by buying privately.

Governments can directly influence the labour market to aid the redistribution of income. The introduction of the National Minimum Wage did much to prevent the payment of poverty wages to certain groups but, perhaps, the greatest impact a government can have is in reducing unemployment. Unemployment is a main cause of people slipping into the bottom income groups and getting the unemployment total down below one million has a considerable effect on the overall distribution of income. The impact would have been even greater if, over the same period, wages at the top end had not been growing rapidly.

The distribution of wealth

Table 11 shows how people hold their wealth, the bulk of it being in life assurance policies and the value of houses owned. A house is, for most people, the most expensive item bought. In recent years house prices have risen strongly but the amount has varied depending on where the houses are located. There was a dip in prices during the early 1990s responding to the recession and high interest rates which created a

Table 11 Composition of net wealth in the household sector

United Kingdom						Percentages
	1987	1991	1996	1997	1998	1999
Life assurance and pension funds	24	27	35	37	37	35
Residential buildings less loans	35	32	23	22	25	26
Securities and shares	10	11	15	16	15	16
Currency and deposits	16	17	16	15	15	14
Non-marketable tenancy rights	9	8	5	5	5	5
Other fixed assets	6	5	4	4	3	3
Other financial assets net of liabilities	1	1	1	1	1	–
Total (=100%) (£ billion at 1999 prices)	2,611	2,913	3,271	3,684	3,955	4,334

Source: Office for National Statistics

situation where some people had borrowed more than their house was worth and so were in negative equity. Otherwise the march in prices has been firmly upwards. The financial sector has become better at selling insurance policies and pensions to private individuals. As incomes increase people seem more prepared to set money aside for old age and have been given tax incentives to do this by the government. Share ownership has also increased boosted by the big privatization offers of the 1980s and 90s.

Wealth represents the value of assets owned but not all of the value of those assets can be realized. Whereas a house can be sold an occupational pension cannot. Table 12 sets out the distribution of marketable wealth.

It is clear that the distribution of wealth is far more unequal than the distribution of income. The bottom 50% of people only own 6% of the wealth of the nation. Also there seems to have been no real redistribution over the years, in fact it has become more unequal. This is significant because the ownership of wealth brings with it additional income earning capacity, so the distribution of wealth contributes to the unequal distribution of income. If the ownership of houses is excluded the picture gets worse. Growing house purchase has spread

Table 12 The distribution of marketable wealth

United Kingdom						Percentages	
	1976	1981	1986	1991	1996	1997	1998
Marketable wealth							
Percentage of wealth owned by adults:							
Most wealthy 1%	21	18	18	17	20	22	23
Most wealthy 5%	38	36	36	35	40	43	44
Most wealthy 10%	50	50	50	47	52	55	56
Most wealthy 25%	71	73	73	71	74	75	75
Most wealthy 50%	92	92	90	92	93	93	94
Total marketable wealth (£ billion)	280	565	955	1,711	2,092	2,280	2,543
Marketable wealth less value of dwellings							
Percentage of wealth owned by adults:							
Most wealthy 1%	29	26	25	29	26	30	26
Most wealthy 5%	47	45	46	51	49	55	50
Most wealthy 10%	57	56	58	64	63	67	65
Most wealthy 25%	73	74	75	80	81	84	86
Most wealthy 50%	88	87	89	93	94	95	95

Source: Inland Revenue

The Wealth List

The richest 10 men and 10 women in the UK for 2000 were:

Men	Wealth	Women	Wealth
1 Hans Rausing Patented the milk carton and runs his own packaging company	£4000m	1 Slavicca Ecclestone	£2000m
2 The Duke of Westminster Inherited most of Mayfair	£3750m	2 Lady Grantchester Daughter of Sir John Moores who founded Littlewoods	£1300m
3 Sir Richard Branson Runs Virgin brands	£2400m	3 Kirsten Rausing Daughter of Gad Rausing, niece of Hans	£1000m
4 Lakshmi Mittal Runs the family steel firm in India	£2200m	4 Ann Gloag Sister of Brian Souter and joint owner of Stagecoach	£565m
4= Lord Sainsbury Supermarket owner	£2200m	5 Freddie Linnet Owns Charles Street Buildings, a Leicester property firm	£390m
5 Bernie and Slavicca Ecclestone Own half of Formula 1	£2000m	6 Paloma Picasso Daughter of the painter, makes jewellery and perfume	£350m
6= Joseph Lewis Founded a leisure and gambling company	£2000m	7 Mary Czernin Inherited 100 acres around Harley Street, London	£300m
8 Sri and Gopi Hinduja Own Gulf Oil	£1950m	8 The Queen Private assets held in shares and estates	£275m
9 Philippe Foriel-Destezet Runs Adecco, the world's largest employment agency	£1500m	9 Josie Rowland Widow of Tiny Rowland, owner of RTZ	£226m
9= Bruno Schroder Family heir of Schroders merchant bank	£1500m	10 Celia Lipton-Farris Widow of American industrialist	£180m

Source: adapted from *The Sunday Times* 'Rich List 2000'

wealth around a little but still about 28% of people claim to have no savings and a further 22% have less than £1500.

Policies to redistribute wealth

Much as we would like to think that it is hard-working people who accumulate most wealth, most of it is, in fact, inherited. The tax on inherited wealth is one of the oldest taxes. It is collected at a time when there is maximum ability to pay and the person who has died doesn't really care what happens. It possesses all the qualities of a good tax. It is convenient in the sense that the taxpayer does have the means to pay the tax, it is certain and cheap to collect. Over the years the tax rates have been reduced in line with the changes in income tax rates and inheritance tax comes with a number of exemptions to allow money and property, except on the largest estates, to be passed on largely tax-free. It is now almost a voluntary tax and raises relatively small amounts of revenue. There are some problems when tax has to be paid on a farm or a business which has to be sold in order to pay the tax bill and there is a view that the tax represents double taxation since tax has already been paid on the money when it was earned. Opposition to the tax is stronger in the USA and one of the first acts of President Bush was to propose the abolition of the $1.6 trillion tax.

Additional taxes are placed on the interest earned from holdings of capital i.e. stamp duties are placed on large asset transactions such as share and house purchases. There have been proposals for a wealth tax but these have never really left the drawing board. It was never politically popular and it could easily become an additional tax on people's income.

Millionaires attack Bush tax cuts

SPECIAL REPORT: GEORGE BUSH'S AMERICA

MARTIN KETTLE IN WASHINGTON

George Bush's massive $1.6 trillion (£1,100bn) tax cut plans are coming under criticism from two groups who would normally be thought of as among his most committed supporters – a number of millionaires and members of the Texas legislature.

The anti-tax cut millionaires are headed by some of America's richest and most famous names, including Warren Buffett, George Soros and Bill Gates Sr, the father of the Microsoft billionaire.

The three are among 120 super-wealthy Americans who are backing a drive organised by Mr Gates Sr against Mr Bush's plan to abolish estate (inheritance) taxes that are paid only by the rich.

"Repealing the estate tax would enrich the heirs of America's millionaires and billionaires while hurting families who struggle to make ends meet," a petition drafted by Mr Gates Sr states.

The billions of dollars in lost government revenue as a result of the plan "will inevitably be made up either by increasing taxes on those less able to pay or by cutting social security, Medicare, environmental protection and many other government programmes so important to our nation's continued well-being", it continues.

Mr Buffett, America's fourth richest man, told the New York Times that he had not yet signed the petition, but only because it did not go far enough in defending "the critical role" of the estate tax. Repealing the tax would be "a terrible mistake", he said.

"Without the estate tax, you in effect will have an aristocracy of wealth, which means you pass down the ability to command the resources of the nation based on heredity rather that merit", he said.

Estate tax is assessed on the net worth of an individual at death. At present it is not payable on the first $675,000 of an estate. Above the threshold, estate tax is paid at 37%, rising to 55% on an upper band of $3m and above. Approximately 2% of Americans pay estate tax and 4,000 Americans provide half of the amount raised by the tax each year.

Backers of the campaign to keep the tax include many other resonant names in American business history, including David Rockefeller and Steven Rockefeller of the oil-based billionaire family.

The elder Mr Gates said he had not yet asked his son to sign his petition, but he revealed that the Microsoft founder was "sympathetic" to the campaign.

The Guardian, 15 February 2001

KEY WORDS	
Income	Quality of life
Flow	Transfer payments
Stock	Flat rate benefits
Lorenz curve	Means tested benefits

Useful websites
Sunday Times Rich List and Pay List www.rhodium.com
The Treasury website www.hm-treasury.gov.uk
The Dept for Social Services website www.dss.gov.uk/ba/

Further reading
Curwen, P., (ed), Chapter 15 in *The UK Economy*, 4th edn, Macmillan, 1997.

Grant, S., and Vidler, C., Part 2 Unit 9 in *Economics in Context*, Heinemann, 2000.

Grant, S., Chapter 23 in Stanlake's *Introductory Economics*, 7th edn, Longman, 2000.

Griffiths, A., and Wall, S., (eds), Chapter 14 in *Applied Economics*, 8th edn, Longman, 1999.

Essay topics
1. (a) Explain why income and wealth are unevenly distributed in the UK. [8 marks]
   (b) Compare the effectiveness of increasing income tax and increasing transfer payments as ways of reducing income inequality. [12 marks]

2. (a) Explain the policies the government might adopt if it wished to achieve a substantial reduction in inequalities in income in the United Kingdom. [20 marks]
   (b) Discuss the view that it is inevitable that measures designed to reduce inequalities in income will adversely affect the performance of the economy. [30 marks]

Source: AQA, Q4, Unit 5, Specimen Paper, 2000.

Data response question
Edexcel, Q3, Paper 3, January 1999

Wage differentials

'A recent Department for Education and Employment (DfEE) report analyses the pattern of pay for two groups of people for whom information on education, family circumstances and jobs in a particular year is available. The data gave a detailed snapshot of a large group of workers in their early thirties in 1978 and a comparable group in 1991. In 1978 men's pay was 64% higher than that of all women employees and 36% higher than that of women in full-time employment. By 1991 these differentials had fallen to 40% and 20% respectively. In 1978 the pay of women in full-time employment was 40% higher than that of women in part-time employment; by 1991 this difference had increased to 52%.

The report looks at all the possible explanations for these changes. A central element of an economist's attempt to explain unequal pay is the notion of human capital. Not surprisingly, improving educational standards turn out to provide part of the explanation for the observed changes in wage differentials. The DfEE paper therefore turns to the next possible theoretical explanation, which is that women and men have different sorts of jobs. Taken together with the human capital explanation, job characteristics help explain a lot more of the wage gap. However, a significant part of the gap between men's and women's pay remains unexplained.

Women in full-time employment represent a valuable resource for employers. This ought to make firms keen to conserve their stock of human capital by introducing family-friendly policies such as flexible working hours, maternity leave and child care. However, the report states that there is a clear trend towards casualisation and a cheap labour strategy. Government policy has favoured this strategy rather than the alternative of maintaining and developing the quality of labour.'

(Adapted from: Diane Coyle, 'The wage gap leaves women in part-time ghettos', *The Independent*, 21 March 1996.)

(a) (i) Explain what is meant by the term 'human capital' (line 13).

[2 marks]

  (ii) Explain why human capital is thought to affect wage differentials between male and female workers.   [5 marks]

(b) Outline two other factors that might explain the differential between the pay of men and women.   [4 marks]

(c) (i) Examine the economic factors which might explain the marked rise in the female participation rate during the past two decades. [8 marks]

   (ii) Discuss two policies which the government might pursue in order to increase the female participation rate still further.
[6 marks]

Chapter Seven

Poverty

'A family is poor if it cannot afford to eat.'
Keith Joseph, a Conservative Government Minister 1982.
'I like flowers.'
The response of Elton John when asked in court why, at one time, he
had spent £298,000 a month on flowers.

Problems of definition

Poverty often can appear to be somebody else's problem and if you
agree with Keith Joseph, it probably is. By his definition, there is no
poverty in the UK but definition is the key to understanding. Poverty is
generally defined in two ways: **absolute and relative poverty**. Absolute
poverty sets a poverty line representing a certain level of income below
which people cannot afford the basic necessities of a healthy life. There
is an attractive 'commonsense' and 'objective' feel to this: simply
identify the necessities, work out their cost and, hey presto, there is
your poverty line. But there are several difficulties with this. What
exactly are these basic necessities? Is a television a necessity or a
luxury? A necessity for one person may be a luxury for another and the
view about what constitutes a necessity will change over time and
between different countries. Some countries such as the USA use a line
to determine government help for the poor and if ever the line is moved
there is a considerable impact upon government expenditure. Hence,
proposals to move the line are resisted. Absolute poverty is important
when reviewing those countries surviving at or near subsistence levels.
Ensuring that the people have enough to eat becomes the major priority
to prevent human suffering. These countries apart, there is a problem in
trying to draw the poverty line and it only appears to have some
meaning if it is related to the existing norms of society.

Relative poverty takes some of these issues into account. Each
society will develop its own view of what poverty means in relation to
what is considered a reasonable and acceptable standard of living. This
will take into account that people need to participate fully in society
and will vary from one country to another. With this definition the UK
does experience some poverty and a way used to measure its extent is to
look at the number of people whose incomes fall more than 50% below
the median income. Approximately 10% of the population fall into this

category or about 5 million people. A problem with this definition is that the poverty target is always shifting as incomes rise and so the eradication of poverty will never be achieved. It also means that the poor in one country could still be relatively rich in international terms.

Taking a global perspective, measuring income levels appears to be a fairly crude measure of poverty since it will fail to take into account factors such as education and health standards, life expectancy and human rights. The United Nations introduced the **Human Development Index (HDI)** in 1990 to cover some of these points and this is calculated annually. Data is collected on life expectancy, educational attainment and GDP and combined into a single figure. With a maximum score of 1, Canada comes closest to perfection scoring 0.96; the UK creeps into the top ten at number 10 just above France, Germany, Denmark and Austria scoring 0.94. At the bottom of the 174 countries comes Sierra Leone at 0.18. A glance at the comparison between the UK and Sierra Leone in 1999 highlights the global inequality that exists.

	Life expectancy (yrs)	Adult Literacy Rate (%)	GDP per person $
UK	77.5	99	21,921
Sierra Leone	37.5	31	260

The gap is further demonstrated by the fact that the poorest 500 million people in the world own less than one tenth of the wealth held by the 200 richest individuals.

The HDI still has its weaknesses. It does not take account of the impact economic activity has on the environment which does have a major effect on people's quality of life. It could be argued that, in the long term, global warming, the depletion of world fish stocks or the spread of BSE should feature far more strongly in any assessment of living standards. Environmental groups are increasingly concerned with sustainability and try to assess the scale of the ecological footprint left by economic activity. The **Index of Sustainable Economic Welfare** does take into account the distribution of welfare, the quantity of voluntary activity and the depletion of resources. There has even been a call for measurement of the **Gross National Happiness** (GNH) from a small Buddhist group in Bhutan.

The causes of global poverty

Countries can be crudely classified into the developed, industrialized and richer countries and the developing, poorer countries although it is important to remember that this is a great over-simplification. Poverty and extreme wealth exist alongside each other in all countries. One important factor influencing the state of development of a country and its level of poverty is its endowment of natural resources. The world's resources are not spread evenly between countries. Some countries have mineral resources, fertile soil and a favourable climate whilst others cope with far more meagre rations of each. The supply and quality of resources lays the foundation for future prosperity. Countries lacking resources often remain poor. It is not surprising that nearly half the population of Sub-Saharan Africa survives on less than a dollar a day.

The pace of population growth is also a concern of poor countries. Often the family is the only source of support for people and so large families are important for survival. But problems occur when the number of births grows rapidly; a greater percentage of the country's population is young, dependent and less productive. In some parts of the world the spread of the AIDS virus is having a devastating effect in causing the premature deaths of millions and leaving large numbers of orphaned children. When a country's reserves are low it finds it difficult to cope with any natural disaster such as flood or drought affecting the fragile ecological structure and these can quickly bring famine and death. Some of the poorer countries such as Bangladesh and Mozambique appear to be suffering from extreme climatic changes resulting from the effects of global warming; a phenomenon largely caused by the polluting activities of the developed countries.

Many of the poorer countries have faced political and economic instability or even civil war making sustained development impossible. If there is no surplus production which can be saved or used for investment in the infrastructure or social capital the result will be a poor education system, a lack of skilled labour and poor communications. In addition, many of the developing countries face a huge debt burden meaning that any surplus that may be achieved has to be paid back to the banks or governments of the rich nations in the form of interest payments.

A comparison of key data in Table 13 showing the UK and Sierra Leone demonstrates the poverty divide.

Table 13 Data profile of the UK and Sierra Leone

Selected data 1999

Indicator	UK	Sierra Leone
Population (m)	59.1	4.9
Life expectancy at birth (yrs)	77.5	37.5
Births per fertile woman	1.7	6.0
Infant mortality rate – deaths under age of 1 per 1000 infants	7.0	169.0
GDP ($)	1.4 trillion	669.4m
Annual growth rate (%)	1.7	–8.1
Agriculture (% of GDP)	1.9	44.4
External debt ($)	–	1.15b

Source: World Bank Group

Reducing global poverty

There are no magic options available. If the poorer countries are to become richer there are only three realistic alternatives. Resources could be transferred from the rich countries to the poor. This is always likely to be difficult because it means trying to persuade the people of the richer nations to accept becoming worse off so that the poor can benefit. There is a strong argument that raising living standards in the poorer countries will actually benefit the rich by creating growing markets for the goods and services produced by the developed countries but this will only occur in the long-term and the rich may not be prepared to wait.

A second alternative is to allow the developed countries to grow but to transfer a larger proportion of the growth in income to the poor. This option is likely to be more attractive to the developed world because the rich are allowed to become richer whilst the poor are encouraged to grow that bit faster so that they gradually catch-up living standards over time. If the economies of the developing countries can be supported so that they can grow faster than the rich then the prosperity gap will be closed.

A third, and most favoured option, is for the rich to give the poor the means to raise their own living standards so that growth is based on much more solid foundations. Given the right mix of resources economic development will begin to take over and the numbers of people living in poverty should decrease.

If the market system is seen to have completely failed the developing countries, a fourth option may gain in attractiveness. Greater state control of assets could direct resources into uses which will create higher growth rates in the future but there may well be political costs if a country chooses this route to prosperity.

Could the economy of Sierra Leone be transformed into looking something like that of the UK, if that is what the people of Sierra Leone want? There is a range of possible strategies:

- Negotiate agreements to end any civil unrest. Political, economic and military stability is essential for economic progress – one immediate benefit is that more resources are freed-up from the military and can be used to raise living standards more directly.
- Introduce more democracy – since the collapse of Communism there seems little alternative. The West and, particularly, the USA like that and are more likely to provide financial support.
- Privatize state-owned assets – encouraging more private initiative will help solve problems and raise money that can be pumped into the health service and education. Again, the USA is a great fan of this.
- Secure a safe water supply and tackle the big killer diseases first – negotiating cheaper supplies of medicine from the major pharmaceutical companies would help.
- Renegotiate any outstanding foreign debt – the lending countries are more likely to consider this if reforms are being undertaken and there is obvious injustice.
- Secure more foreign aid if it is to be used to boost investment and is lent on the borrower's terms – too often loans have been given for the benefit of the donor country rather than the borrower.
- Welcome foreign trans-national companies into your country in some form of partnership – this will create jobs and give the government a chance of holding onto control of key parts of the economy. Another benefit may be gaining access to new technology but care is needed: the trans-nationals have huge economic power and the turnover of some of them is greater than the national income of many smaller countries.
- Give high priority to boosting education with universal schooling for all and especially for women. This will lead to increased skills so that higher value work will be attracted and help to keep population growth under control.
- Introduce State support for the elderly as soon as possible to ease the need to rely totally on families – family size may fall. Rising living and education standards and effective economic policies

together with easier access to contraception will help to keep population growth under control.

- Move to higher value-added production when possible – most of the value of food products comes at the processing stage and the developing countries could take on more of this.
- If the country produces raw materials or agricultural commodities, join with other producers to try to get a grip on the market and use some monopoly power against the international buyers of the major retail chains.
- Introduce greater diversification into the economy – many developing countries run into problems because they are over dependent on individual crops and so destroyed by crop failure or collapsing prices.
- Open up to more international trade and seek easier access into the more profitable high income markets of Western Europe and North America – this could be difficult at first but more competition will encourage domestic producers to become more efficient and will also make available cheaper imports. Selective protection may be needed for a short transition phase.

The reality is far more difficult and complex than this simple list suggests. Countries may find themselves in a cycle of poverty where it is extremely difficult to break through and achieve a leap in living standards. Some countries do achieve it. The newly industrialized countries of the Far East such as Korea and Taiwan have grown rapidly in recent years. If a developing country is able to achieve growth rates, which are twice those of the developed nations, then they should be able to catch up living standards over a period of 20–30 years.

Poverty in the UK

Pockets or even suitcases of poverty exist in the UK and the record on this is not without blemish. 14 million people live on less than half the average income, a total that has been growing in recent years, and 5 million live in absolute poverty. In 2000 Britain was 19th out of 23 industrial countries in terms of children living in relative poverty and had 30% of children living in absolute poverty compared to less than 5% in Sweden. 2.7 million households live in poor housing conditions and nearly 500,000 people are homeless. The poor are more likely to suffer from ill-health, have greater difficulties in child birth, will die on average eight years before more affluent groups and are four times more likely to commit suicide. A Breadline Europe investigation declared that 17% of the population felt that their income was below that needed to buy the basic necessities of life although this number would have fallen with more recent government initiatives.

Cracking UK poverty

There are two theories that attempt to explain why poverty still exists today. One view is that the poor themselves are to blame. They are somehow socially deviant, work-shy, dependent on benefits and refuse to take advantage of the opportunities presented to them. They form an **underclass** excluded from the normal social expectations of society. If this is correct then there is little that a government can do to reduce poverty: it is a matter for the individual. Removing the cushion of benefits and adjusting tax incentives may have the effect of persuading more people to take greater responsibility for their own welfare. Advocates of the free market would latch onto this as confirmation of a non-interventionist approach; it is for the poor to get themselves out of their current position.

Alternatively, poverty can be seen as being the result of the way society is structured. Certain groups lose out in education, health, housing and all other aspects of society and so are not able to benefit to the same extent as others. It is not the fault of the individual; it is much more to do with the system within which they have grown up. If this is the case then governments can do a lot to reduce poverty. The whole thrust of recent government policy to tackle 'social exclusion', to improve standards in education, improve access to health care as well as policies to encourage people back into employment and the introduction of the National Minimum Wage and raising benefits indicate a government desire to address the economic barriers society places before people who wish to increase their own living standards. Indeed, the government has chosen to set targets for the reduction of child poverty over the next 20 years.

Today it is easy to assume that everybody has the same life-chances but, unfortunately, life is not like Hollywood and the chances of winning the National Lottery are still 14 million to one.

KEY WORDS

Absolute poverty	Gross National Happiness
Relative poverty	Underclass
Human Development Index	Social exclusion
Index of Sustainable Economic Welfare	

Useful websites
World Bank www.//devdata.worldbank.org
Department of Sociology, Lancaster University
  www.comp.lancs.ac.uk/sociology
World Bank www.worldbank.org
The Union of Concerned Scientists site
  www.ucsusa.org/environment/pop/faq.html

Further reading
Atkinson, B., Livesey, F., and Milward, R., Chapter 9 in *Applied Economics*, Macmillan, 1998.

Curwen, P., (ed), Chapter 16 in *The UK Economy*, 4th edn, Macmillan, 1997.

Grant, S., and Vidler, C., Part 2 Unit 10 in *Economics in Context*, Heinemann, 2000.

Griffiths, A., and Wall, S., (ed), Chapter 14 in *Applied Economics*, 8th edn, Longman, 1999.

Essay topics
1. 'The government's strategy is based around moving people from welfare and into work and making work pay' (HM Treasury).
    (a) Explain how the tax and benefit system may affect work incentives. [10 marks]
    (b) Discuss whether reform of the tax and benefit system alone can be expected to reduce income inequality and poverty in the UK. [15 marks]

    Source: OCR, Q3, Specimen Paper 2884, 2000.

2. (a) Explain how relative poverty can increase whilst absolute poverty falls. [8 marks]
    (b) Discuss policies to reduce world poverty. [12 marks]

Data response question
Edexcel, Q1, Unit 5A, Specimen Paper, 2000

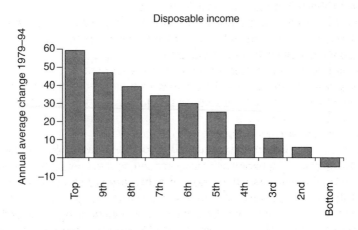

Disposable income

What is poverty? For Labour, the fact that the lower quarter or so of earners are becoming worse off compared with others means that poverty is increasing. The party points to the fact that the number of people in households earning less than half the average income — a common European definition of poverty — has increased from less than 5 million in 1979 to some 14 million now. The Tories, they charge, have therefore pitched 9 million more people into the ranks of the poor.

Nonsense, say the Conservatives. Relative definitions of poverty are meaningless. By that measure a desperately poor country that distributes its squalor evenly would have no poverty. It is much better to look at real incomes and living standards. These show that those Britons who earn the least have a bit more cash, and many more creature comforts, than they did in 1979.

Consider Labour's case first. Inequality has increased in Britain since 1979, and faster than in any OECD country except America. So it is not surprising that the number of people earning less than half the average income has increased, to almost one-quarter of the population. Labour is also correct that the toughest kind of poverty, namely homelessness, has increased. It is also true that those living on state benefits have a meagre time of it. According to the most recent report from the Department of Social Security, the 10% of people on the lowest incomes have seen their real incomes fall by 13% since 1979. The other 90% saw an improvement.

On a philosophical level, Labour thinkers like Frank Field, a backbench

MP, argue that the increased use of means-testing – which is applied twice as often as before 1979 – has undesirable effects. Means-tests trigger 'poverty traps' that make work or saving uneconomic, and 'moral hazards' that encourage people to lie or cheat.

The Tories interpret economic history differently. Yes, they concede, inequality has increased, but they claim an employment record that looks good compared with the rest of Europe's.

Letting people price themselves into the labour market, even at low wages, means they have a chance to work their way up the economic ladder. Many do just that. Three-quarters of a surveyed sample of 89,051 men aged under 45 (and 905 of those in the bottom tenth by income) had higher real incomes in 1994 than they did in 1979.

And yes, Tories further concede, means-testing is problematic, but it has helped to target benefits to those in need, and to contain the growth in public spending. As for the government's alleged stinginess, since 1979 there has been an 86% increase in social spending in real terms, to more than £90 billion a year. While the income after housing costs for the lowest 10% seems to have declined, few of those who were in the bottom tenth in 1979 have stayed there ever since. Most of them have moved up.

Moreover, there is more income in the bottom tenth than official surveys can account for. Spending surveys find that this group, which is notoriously difficult to track, had increased its median expenditure by 28% at a time when its real income was supposed to have been falling. The proportion of lower-income households that have cars, video-recorders, central heating, washing machines and other consumer goods has increased markedly. The poor, therefore, cannot be called poorer simply because other income groups saw their salaries fatten faster. They have become richer in visible ways.

By their chosen standards, both Tories and Labour are right. If inequality is the most important measure of economic health, then Britain is worse off than it was in 1979. If income and a colour television are better indicators, then just about everyone is better off. The exceptions are the homeless and those who were in the bottom 10% in 1979 and have stayed there ever since.

Labour faces a different issue. It has been quick to damn inequality, but slow to propose remedies. Tony Blair does not talk about redistributive taxation. A high minimum wage could narrow the gap a little, but it could also price some people out of work and force them into idleness and dependence.

(Source: 'The worse off but richer', *The Economist Election Briefing,* © The Economist Newspaper Limited, London, 1997)

(a) With reference to the information provided, comment on the significance of the distinction between absolute and relative poverty. [10 marks]

(b) The distribution of income has become more uneven since 1979. Discuss the validity of this statement. [10 marks]

(c) Examine two policies that might be employed to reduce the inequality in the distribution of income. [20 marks]

(d) Evaluate the proposition that an increase in inequality is a necessary condition for raising the rate of economic growth. [20 marks]

Chapter Eight

After work

'*When I'm 64.*'
The Beatles

Both old age and death have two things in common: we don't believe they will happen to us and we don't like talking about them. The law of averages suggests that we will die and population data informs us that more and more people are living into old age and likely to survive into their 70s, 80s and 90s. This will have a major effect on the way the economy operates. Table 14 illustrates the changes to the age structure of population.

Comparing the population changes over the last century it is clear that there has been a major shift in the age distribution of population. A

Table 14 The age structure of the UK population

United Kingdom									Percentages
	Under 16s	16 – 24	25 – 34	35 – 44	45 – 54	55 – 64	65 – 74	75 and over	All ages (=100%) (millions)
Males									
1901[1]	33.6	19.7	15.7	12.2	8.8	5.8	3.1	1.2	18.5
1931[1,2]	25.6	17.8	15.9	13.0	11.9	9.2	5.0	1.7	22.1
1961[1]	24.8	13.9	13.1	13.9	13.9	11.2	6.3	3.1	25.5
1991	21.4	13.7	16.3	14.1	11.6	10.0	8.0	4.8	28.2
1998	21.3	11.4	16.2	14.7	13.3	9.9	7.9	5.3	29.1
Females									
1901[1]	31.4	19.6	16.4	12.2	9.0	6.2	3.6	1.6	19.7
1931[1,2]	23.0	17.0	16.0	14.0	12.5	9.3	5.7	2.4	24.0
1961[1]	22.1	12.9	12.1	13.2	13.7	12.0	8.7	5.3	27.3
1991	19.3	12.5	15.1	13.4	11.1	10.0	9.5	9.0	29.6
1998	19.6	10.5	15.0	14.0	12.9	9.9	8.9	9.3	30.1

[1] Figures for 1901, 1931 and 1961 relate to age bands under 15 and 15–24.
Figures for 1901 and 1931 are Census enumerated; figures for later years are mid-year estimates.
[2] 1931 figures for Northern Ireland relate to the 1937 Census.
Source: Office for National Statistics; General Register Office for Scotland; Northern Ireland Statistics and Research Agency

lower **birth rate** has caused declining numbers of under 16s. The fastest growing age groups have been the over 65s where there are over three times the numbers at the end of the century as there were at the start and this trend is likely to continue in the 21st Century. 18% of the population, 10.7 million people, is over pensionable age rising to 11.9 million by 2021. The UK has an **ageing population** and this brings with it certain economic problems. Older people require more medical treatment and make more demands on the health service so more resources are needed which may mean higher taxation. The pattern of demand for goods and services changes causing a need for resources to be redeployed. Housing needs change with a greater number of single person households, more sheltered housing and care homes. The workforce becomes a little less dynamic and adaptable to new technologies which may impact upon the enterprise shown within the economy.

As people move beyond the retirement age they become part of the **dependent population** and become reliant on the workforce to produce the goods and services which generate the rising standards of living for all. Older people still have wants and needs but are no longer able to, or choose not to, satisfy those needs from their own current earnings. As more people move into this group a larger burden is placed on the working population to generate the tax revenues that can be used to provide the state pensions offered to those over retiring age.

Pensions

In principle, pensions are a form of savings which are accumulated during the working lifetime and is then paid back to the savers as income when they retire. The funds for the state pension are collected from **National Insurance Contributions**, a broadly proportional tax levied on employees and employers with the government encouraging this form of savings by giving tax relief on the amounts saved. In practice, it is the contributions of the current workforce which pay for the pensions of those now over retiring age: it is a pay-as-you-go scheme. Most of us believe that by paying into a pension scheme we are ensuring that we will be able to enjoy a comfortable standard of living for the rest of our lives. The reality is less reassuring.

The amount of state pension each person receives is dependent on the number of years he/she has contributed. The system works on the basis that men retiring at 65 will have paid their contributions for a maximum of 44 **qualifying years**, women retiring at 60 will have contributed for a maximum of 39 years (the retiring ages for men and women are being brought into line over the period 2010–20 by which time both sexes will be expected to retire at 65). To gain a full pension people need to have contributed for the full number of qualifying years and will receive a proportion of the full rate depending on how many years have been missed. For married women this is a serious issue since many have chosen to opt out of the full payments only to find that, by retiring age, they have under-provided for themselves. The system means that when we reach retiring age we are all entitled to draw our state pension at some level which can be topped up with the Government's **Minimum Income Guarantee (MIG)**, a means-tested benefit related to the amount of savings held. In 2001 the basic state pension for single people is £72.50 per week rising to £75.50 in 2002. Married couples receive £115.90 rising to £120.70. With the MIG income levels rise to £92.15 and £140.55 respectively.

The basic state pension is regarded as a bare minimum and people are encouraged to pay into other pension schemes to boost their retirement income. There is the **State Earnings Related Pension Scheme (SERPS)** (becoming the **State Second Pension** after 2002) which people can contract out of in favour of private schemes which may be provided by employers through **occupational pensions**, private pension providers or **stakeholder pensions**, a new scheme offered with low costs designed for lower income earners.

The difficulty from the government's point of view is that the cost of pension provision rises with the growth in the numbers of pensioners and with any arrangement to link the level of pension to the index of retail prices or the average rises in wages. Governments are reluctant to enter agreements that, potentially, can create escalating government expenditure over which they have no control. The other problem here is that the state pension on its own will only be able to give pensioners a good standard of living if the basic pension rate is raised considerably.

The government is presented with some difficult choices. It could choose to keep pension rates low to keep expenditure in check but risk losing the votes of pensioners at election time; introduce a means-tested pension for the long-term but destroy the insurance element of the pension itself; increase pensions in line with inflation but make every effort to keep inflation rates low; increase pensions in line with average earnings which may require even higher expenditure and higher taxes or encourage people to make more private provision for their own pension and to regard the state pension as providing for the very basic needs.

Pensioners favour re-establishing the link with average earnings which was withdrawn in 1980. It is estimated that pensions would be about one third higher than they are at the present time if this link had been maintained. One difficulty is that linking pensions to the retail prices index may not be selecting the appropriate index. The RPI is calculated based on the spending of the average family. Pensioners spend their money in a different way and spend a much greater proportion on housing, fuel and food. This means that if these products rise in price faster than the average the living standards of the old will fall causing further hardship.

Governments tend to prefer to set a reasonable basic pension but encourage people to make additional provision themselves. In voting terms the grey vote will become more significant. Older people are more likely to vote in greater numbers and so governments may well need to respond to grey demands if they wish to be re-elected.

Pensions are a type of saving we all need to consider and the earlier the better. The aim is to build up a large enough lump sum to generate sufficient income to maintain you at an acceptable level when you no longer have income or want to be earning yourself. The evidence is that people under-provide for themselves. 40% of pensioners live on less than £10,000 per year and 57% wish they had planned for their future better. The problem is **opportunity cost**. A decision to save means that a person foregoes the immediate benefits of spending that money. Old age is a long way off and so many people ignore the call of the pension but this can be costly. A person wanting to receive an income of £15,000 on retirement needs to save about £230 a month if they start in their twenties. If they leave it to their forties they need to save £450 a month. The result for many is relative poverty in old age.

The demographic time bomb

The growth in the older population and the decline in birth rate are features of most countries across the developed world. The population of the EU currently represents approximately 6% of the world's population but this will reduce to 4% in 25 years and then the EU's population will fall. This is good in some respects. There will be less people consuming scarce resources and the impact on the environment will lessen although numbers in the developing world are expanding rapidly. However, there are problems. There will be a reduction in the size of the workforce which will result in lower growth rates and higher tax burdens especially where countries have developed generous pension arrangements such as in Germany and Italy. If pension levels are to be maintained then there will have to be higher taxes or increased levels of borrowing from governments which may be against the requirements of the EU. Alternatively, pension provision can be scaled down with private schemes taking more of the burden, the retirement

Age time bomb may just be a squib

ROSS DAVIES, EVENING STANDARD

The 'demographic time bomb' could turn out to be a damp squib, given a bit of careful handling, say people who count – the actuaries – or those arithmeticians who say they can make financial sense of the future.

Actuary Fiona Matthews recently calculated that in 1951, the Queen would have had to write 300 birthday messages to centenarians, 4400 by 1991, and by the time she herself were to reach the ton-up, in 2027, she could have up to 32,000 stamps to be licked.

Since the beginning of the 20th century, life expectancy at birth has risen by about half, from around 45 for men and 49 for women, to 74 and 79. Old age pensions were introduced in 1911. You had to be 70 to qualify, an age you only reached in those days if you didn't need the money anyway.

Today, however, the Cabinet Office calculates, a third of people between the age of 50 and retirement age (65 for men, 60 for women) are not working. And for about half of these early retirers, State benefits are the main income.

Another actuary, Brian Ridsdale, says there are 3.5 working people to 'support' each person over pensionable age: by the time the Queen became a centenarian herself, the female pensionable age will have been raised from 60 to 65, but the number of 'supporters' per retiree will still be on the way down to 2.4.

State pensioners will no doubt object to the suggestion that they are being 'supported' by people still in work, but that, says Ridsdale, is what is happening. 'The State pension scheme is 'pay-as-you-go', which means that your contributions are being spent to pay somebody else's pension today, not set aside to pay your pension tomorrow.'

But what if the younger generation decides it doesn't want to pay up for its parents as today's is doing now? That is one of the 'what ifs?' pondered by members of the Institute of Actuaries and its Scottish counterpart, the Faculty of Actuaries.

Ridsdale chairs the IoA/FoA ageing population group, which has been tinkering with this time bomb, and he concludes it contains some highly unstable and nasty stuff. Perhaps the worst ingredient, actuarially speaking, is a delayed-action poverty device, designed to hit all those good-lifers, corporate burn-outs and others who take early retirement. 'Too many early retirers take a lump sum as part of their pension pay-off, settle a few debts, and then live to see what is left become too little to live upon,' Ridsdale says.

Even so, economists as well as actuaries point out, there will be increasing inequality between those who retire on company or private pensions and those who rely solely upon the State.

The good news, the actuaries say, is that Britain can contain the blast, if not defuse it altogether. The demographic time bomb need not blow Britain's GDP out of the water over the next 50 years. Productivity has been rising at 2% a year for years, for example, and that should be more than enough to cover the cost of the aged without undue economic problems.

The real problem is not that Britain may become an impoverished nation, but that it will stay being, in pension matters, a stupid one. In Canada, Ridsdale points out, it is now possible to raise pension contributions because politicians have set out the problems sensibly, and the electorate has decided it will bite the bullet. 'In the UK, however, Government, the media, the health and the insurance industry could do much more to research the impact an ageing population could have, and then put everybody in the picture so some sensible decisions can be reached in time to see off trouble, and reached with the support of the people who will have to pay for those decisions – the public.'

Evening Standard, 9 November 2000

age could be raised to reduce the demand for pensions and the size of the workforce could be increased by reducing unemployment and encouraging growth in economic activity so that more people get back into the workforce.

The UK government has adopted all of these approaches. The link to average earnings was broken in 1980 so that pensions rise more slowly in line with retail prices. The government has attempted to create stability so that economic growth is encouraged. Unemployment has fallen and more of the economically inactive, particularly lone parents, have been attracted back into the workforce. Incentives have been given to people to take greater responsibility for their own pension provision. The retirement age for women is being raised in line with men and some work is being done to combat age discrimination to allow people to continue working for as long as they are physically able. Other EU countries have not yet addressed the problem and face a rising pension demand which will threaten their ability to act with economic independence.

KEY WORDS

Birth rate
Ageing population
Dependent population
National Insurance
    Contributions
Qualifying years
Minimum Income Guarantee

State Earnings Related Pension
    Scheme
State Second Pension
Occupational pension
Stakeholder pension
Opportunity cost

Useful websites

National Statistics site
   www.statistics.gov.uk./nsbase/learningzone/population.asp
Department of the Environment, Transport and the Regions
www.housing.detr.gov.uk
More national statistics www.statistics.gov.uk/.nsbase/learningzone
Age Concern England, Cymru, Northern Ireland, Scotland
   www.ace.org.uk

Further reading

Anderton, A., Unit 76 in *Economics*, 3rd edn, Causeway Press, 2000.
Ball, J., Chapter 5 in *The British Economy at the Crossroads*, Financial Times/Pitman Publishing, 1998.

Curwen, P., (ed), Chapter 14 in *The UK Economy*, 4th edn, Macmillan, 1997.

Littlewood, M., Chapters 4–10 in *How to Create a Competitive Market in Pensions*, IEA, 1998.

Karen Dunnell, *Policy Responses to Population Ageing and Population Decline – UK*, UN

Essay topics

1. 'Over the next 35 years, the proportion of the world's population aged sixty and over will nearly double from 9 per cent to 16 per cent. If they are to provide adequately for people's needs, pension systems must be changed, although the changes may be slow and, in some cases, painful.'
   (a) Explain the features of a good pension system. [8 marks]
   (b) Discuss the economic difficulties that countries are likely to face as they try to change pension systems to cope with ageing populations. [12 marks]

2. (a) Discuss the consequences of an ageing population. [8 marks]
   (b) Assess three policies for reducing the growth of government expenditure on state pensions. [12 marks]

   Source: OCR, Q2, Paper 4387, June 2000.

Data response question

OCR, Q1, Paper 4387, June 1998

Current Labour Market Issues in Singapore

As a result of persistently high GDP growth rates since the mid-1970s, Singapore has long enjoyed virtually full employment. Moreover, this outstanding economic success has been achieved without any of the adverse side-effects often experienced by many western countries, such as the UK, when employment rises beyond certain levels.

Increasingly, however, prosperous Singaporeans prefer to work in offices rather than in factories or on building sites. The resulting shortage of workers in labour-intensive manufacturing and construction industries has led local companies to rely heavily on recruiting from less affluent and less urbanised regions of South East Asia.

Government policies have tried to balance the demand for foreign labour and the problems that can be created by a large influx of overseas workers. For example, manufacturing and construction firms hiring foreign manual workers have to pay a tax on each overseas employee and there is a ceiling on the number of such workers that each company is allowed to employ.

The ageing of Singapore's population (Table 1) creates further problems including that of how to ensure that Singaporeans are adequately provided for on their retirement from work.

Table 1 Singaporean Workers aged 40 years and above
1980–2030

| Year | | Workers aged 40 and above | |
		Number	Per cent of total workforce
1980		282,800	26.5
1990		472,000	32.1
2000	Estimates	654,000	43.0
2010	"	756,200	48.6
2020	"	762,700	49.4
2030	"	791,500	52.9

The Singaporean state retirement pensions system is classified as a funded scheme unlike the 'pay-as-you-go' system in the UK, which is essentially a simple tax-transfer scheme. Singapore's Central Provident Fund (CPF) is a compulsory savings scheme whereby both the employer and the employee make monthly contributions to a fund which is managed by an independent national board. Savings accumulate in each individual employee's CPF account and may be withdrawn at the age of 55 to finance retirement or, at any age, for approved uses such as buying property or paying for education, training and health care.

(a) (i) Use the information provided to identify why Singapore relies on foreign labour. [2 marks]

  (ii) State and explain one economic problem that might be created by the movement of large numbers of foreign workers into an urban environment like Singapore. [2 marks]

(b) Describe one adverse side effect 'often experienced by western countries, such as the UK, when employment rises beyond certain levels'. [2 marks]

(c) (i) Use a diagram to explain how the tax on foreign workers is likely to affect the short run average total costs of a typical Singapore-based manufacturing company. [3 marks]

  (ii) How would you expect Singapore-based manufacturing companies to react to this tax in the short run and in the long run? [4 marks]

(d) To what extent does the data in Table 1 indicate that Singapore has an ageing population? [2 marks]
(e) Discuss the advantages and disadvantages of a funded pension scheme such as that adopted in Singapore. [5 marks]

Chapter Nine

Future trends

'Rail travel at high speed is not possible because passengers, unable to breathe, would die of asphyxia.'
Dr Dionysus Lardner (1793–1859) Professor of Natural Philosophy and Astronomy at University College, London

It is notoriously difficult to forecast the future and yet economists continue to make a living by convincing people that they have the ability to do just that. By analyzing past performance, constructing models and theories the economist hopes to be able to predict the consequences of actions. Can such visionary qualities be brought to the labour market? Some trends are clear but others are open to a wide range of speculation.

The market for labour

The fundamentals of supply and demand influencing wage levels are unlikely to change but some characteristics of the market will alter. It has already been noted that the supply of labour is changing. The workforce is getting older with a greater proportion of people leaving the labour market in their 50s. There is a tension here. People are living longer, staying fitter and keeping active and may not have planned financially for an extended retirement. Some may need to keep working and the age of retirement may become more flexible. Certainly firms will need to consider making use of older workers because a declining birth rate will reduce the supply of younger employees. Vibrancy within the workforce will emerge from the rising numbers of immigrant workers and, over time after the initial xenophobic fears, these people should become more highly valued members of society. Much may depend on the prevailing political inclinations of the British people with the hope being that the British retain their tolerant, outward looking, internationalist attitude rather than becoming sour, inward looking and suspicious of anybody from further east than Southend.

The **economic activity rate of women workers** will continue to increase. Women are achieving higher qualifications in school, going on to university and are, rightly, expecting to be able to build a worthwhile career. The growth in divorces and numbers of lone parents has increased the demand for equal treatment at work but it is still the case that equality of wages is a long way off. Further legislation may be necessary to persuade firms to monitor wage levels seriously and to address the problem if unexplained inequality exists. A tighter labour market could also do much to assist the fight for equality when employers are prepared to push up wages to attract workers. Equality in the home is more elusive with women doing 70% of housework even when they are going out to work.

In the future the UK should be producing more highly skilled workers to match our closest competitors. School standards should continue to rise with the attention being given to ensure that all school leavers possess the basic employability skills and nearly 50% of school leavers will go on to higher education. The problem for these people will be that the increase in supply of well-qualified graduates will push up the requirements of careers. Graduates may well be forced to study beyond a degree or be willing to take on jobs previously offered to those with lower qualifications. However, there are still likely to be shortages of people with IT and entrepreneurial skills.

On the demand side, employers will be seeking different skills as technology and work patterns change. A concerted effort led by the government should lead to the raising of skills levels and a recognition of the importance of lifelong learning. Expansion will occur in the numbers of call centres and Internet trading should establish itself. Successful Internet dot coms should see rapid expansion in the new **knowledge-based economy** but there will be the inevitable shakeout of Internet companies who fail to find the secret of converting Internet business into profits. Moves towards the 24-hour society will continue requiring a more flexible workforce as people are expected to work more less-sociable hours although, overall, the number of hours worked will move towards the European average. The speed at which jobs in manufacturing disappear may depend on the success in improving the productivity of the UK workforce, the value of the exchange rate and whether a decision to join the Euro is taken. This is, perhaps, the major economic decision on the horizon. Public opinion has strongly supported the retention of the pound and the government will have a difficult task if it wishes to turn that around. It is doubtful whether the argument can be carried purely on the economics of the issue. The march towards **globalization** seems unstoppable and will also bring its threats to the manufacturing sector. Capital and, particularly, the new technology are highly mobile and will seek out parts of the world with low labour costs and little regulation.

Work is becoming less secure. With flatter organizational structures firms load more responsibility on employees bringing extra stress and

No more nine to five

RICHARD REEVES

Long hours, low pay and a crushing lack of job security … In Britain, it seems, we love to whinge about work. But as Richard Reeves of the Industrial Society reports, most of us have never had it so good.

Stress, sleeplessness, depression, heart disease, shortness of temper, memory loss, irritable bowel syndrome, anxiety, marital breakdown, child delinquency, impotence, the decline of local neighbourhoods, cancer, RSI, rudeness, suicide, Tins couples (Two Incomes, No Sex) – a mere shortlist of some of the symptoms of the postmodern malaise.

The cause of all our woes? Enter, stage right, the prime suspect – work. Wicked, wicked work. An avalanche of surveys, polls and expert commentaries show that we all work too long, too hard, that our bosses are beastly, that we are insecure and afraid. You know all this stuff. We seem to be workers on the verge of a nervous breakdown.

A council housing officer wins £67,000 from her employers for workplace stress; a young, gifted surgeon works 220 hours in 10 days, then breaks into a stranger's bungalow, strips naked and bites anyone who tries to help him; a financial services company enrolls its overworked staff on to a dating agency's books; Businesswoman of the Year Nikki Beckett says she keeps her weekends clear for her children – but puts in 70 hours a week for her company NSB Retail Systems; Longbridge lives, but Dagenham dies.

So far, so bad. But there's plenty of good news about work, too – even if it is not always shared with the same enthusiasm as the 'Work Sucks' stories. The average wage has increased 57 per cent in the past decade. The proportion of firms offering maternity leave in excess of the statutory minimum has quintupled over the same time period. A third of firms now offer sabbaticals; two-thirds allow staff to work from home some of the time. Four out of 10 UK workers declare themselves 'very satisfied' with their jobs, more than in France, Germany, Italy or Spain.

An infant-school dinner lady wins the Lottery but – like many of her fellow winners – keeps working. 'I love my job because I enjoy talking to the children and parents,' she said. 'It is a very responsible job.' A young woman is crowned Miss Northern Ireland and refuses to give up her admin job in a doctor's surgery. 'I love my job,' she explained. Unemployment plumbs record lows – and may even drop below the symbolic 1 million mark before long. We seem to have never had it so good.

The Observer, 23 July 2000

pressure. Part-time working, split shifts, temporary contracts and performance-related pay also carry pressure. Apart from back pains, stress is developing as the most common work-related illness and yet we are generally better off with more to spend and the aspiration of full employment in sight. Work patterns over a working life will be more varied. People will change their jobs more often and possibly experience spells of unemployment in between. Keeping skills up-to-date will be essential. The trade unions can make a significant contribution here in contributing to the efforts to improve the basic skills of the workforce and lifelong learning. They are still relatively weak in the new economy but with economic expansion, falling unemployment, the minimum wage and a generally supportive government the trade unions should welcome a new period of growth in membership and influence.

Employment patterns

The process of **de-industrialization** will continue with a further rise in service sector employment and decline in manufacturing although it is likely that the pace will slow. This is largely due to the fact that most of the major manufacturing plants have already been hit hard and the UK is left with a slimmer but more efficient remainder which will be able to cope better with future uncertainty. The prospects for manufacturing will depend on UK firms exploiting their advantages in hi-tech production and the possible entry to the Euroland. **EU enlargement** to the east also brings threats as countries with low wage costs such as the Czech Republic, Poland and Hungary prove attractive locations for new manufacturing plants.

The **employment rate** is also likely to continue to increase as the government further improves the incentives for people to get back into the workforce. This will particularly affect lone parents, women and older workers. The changing demographics will force companies to look at older workers as a fruitful labour supply source. The Internet will make a bigger impact on job searching and will ensure that good labour market information is available to all. Quick access to opportunities will be available and this should have the effect of opening up labour markets across Europe to UK residents although the actual number taking advantage is still likely to remain small.

The concept of a **'natural' rate of unemployment** will continue to recede in importance as unemployment continues to fall even with a greater level of regulation. Government policy emphasis will continue to focus on the supply side of the economy to create a more productive and adaptable workforce. The reduction in unemployment has brought its rewards in that lower government spending on this area has allowed large chunks of National Debt to be repaid reducing the interest payments which can then be targeted on further areas of need such as schools and hospitals. Governments of all persuasions have been hooked into a low tax regime relying on growth of the economy to fund extra welfare spending. A potential problem for Chancellors here is that if a government under-spends there may be a demand from taxpayers for them to have their money paid back to them and so there could follow demands for further tax cuts. There is a danger that the self-interest of taxpayers could override the responsibility of governments to ensure that the tax system also embraces the concept of equity or fairness.

Income distribution and poverty

Many fine words have been spoken about this issue. The logic of providing greater help to the poor and underprivileged seems undisputable but any progress is painfully slow. The elimination of child poverty is an admirable target but still approximately 250 million children aged 5–14 are employed across the world, often in very poor working conditions. International debt remains a huge burden on the poor and preventable disease kills millions. The ambition is clear and individual countries and charities do make a significant impact on particular areas but too often the help is channelled into disaster relief just to keep people alive or provided for the benefit of the donor countries. Global businesses do have a responsibility to ensure that their working practices do not offend standards of human decency but the consensus needed in the developed world to initiate a larger transfer of resources is not there yet.

Within the UK, a clutch of policies exist to reduce the income gap and these are adopted with different degrees of enthusiasm by governments. High rates of progressive taxation on income have been abandoned as ways of increasing funds for redistribution with governments preferring to introduce indirect taxes, sometimes called stealth taxes, which are less visible and therefore more politically attractive. Policies have been favoured which target the poor by providing benefits where they are needed but also encourage them into work so that they can support themselves. New arrangements to encourage people to make adequate provision for their old age will help tackle poverty by targeting pensioner households. Many of these changes are a direct response to the **demographic time bomb** and the UK appears to be in a far better position to prevent the massive explosion which may well hit some other European countries.

The **North/South 'divide'** continues to raise hackles. A UK economic growth rate of 2.5% (as predicted in the 2001 Budget) seems promising but it is an average. If the bulk of that growth is concentrated in London and the South East, other parts of the country can still be left in

Battle for survival in a divided country

MENDING the North-South Divide is one of the greatest challenges facing Tony Blair. While the South-East enjoys the fruits of rising prosperity, Labour's heartland is hurting as badly now as it ever did under the Tories.

The thorniest problem facing the South is where to build the 1.1 million new homes it will need by 2016.

Meanwhile, at the other end of England, manufacturing jobs are draining inexorably away as traditional markets dry up and a strong pound makes exports increasingly uncompetitive.

Despite New Labour's attempts to heal the rift between North and South that appeared during the Thatcher era, unless something more is done it threatens to become a gaping chasm by the next General Election.

In the South-East, unemployment is falling steadily. In the North-East the figures are static and have even risen slightly. According to Government statistics almost one-in-four homes in this region are now officially classed as "poor". That compares with just one in ten households in the South-East.

The problem is easy to see but difficult to solve. The North-East economy still relies too heavily on manufacturing industry.

The miners may have gone, the shipyards may be pale shadows of their former glory but the region still has more working people in manufacturing than any other area apart from the Midlands.

Critics blame the Government's economic policy. Despite the Chancellor's tight rein on spending, the economy continues to be dogged by two persistent problems: an erratic exchange rate and continued inflationary pressure, with wages and spending rising too fast.

This has been fuelled primarily in the South where already steep house prices have accelerated dramatically in the past year. Rising wages have also increased spending power, only last month high street spending rose spectacularly as wealthy shoppers clamoured to buy a new kind of video games console. The southern economy is awash with money for such frivolous purchases, further stoking inflationary pressures.

If left unchecked, the net result of this will be to create a boom that cannot last.

The Bank of England's Monetary Policy Committee hopes to dampen inflationary pressures by adjusting interest rates. This, in turn, leads to a stronger pound.

Manufacturers – of which the North-East has a disproportionate amount – find themselves hobbled by higher costs and unable to compete abroad because their goods cost too much. These were the reasons cited by the Hong Kong company Onwa for pulling the plug on its Tyneside TV factory last month.

As a result, high value segments such as aerospace and electronics in the South are experiencing a genuine recovery. Basic materials, textiles and traditional heavy engineering, in the North, are still languishing in the doldrums.

The Northern Echo, 10 November 1999

decline. The geographical pull of the markets of the EU will continue to favour development in the South East and the absence of a fast and efficient rail network also contributes to the divide. But there are pressures in the opposite direction as people seek a better quality of life offered outside the capital. Some regional centres such as Leeds and Manchester are booming and providing a focus for wider regeneration, just look around at the work done to revive the water frontage in our major cities. One of the key issues is the way in which economic policy is often perceived as addressing the needs of the South East with high interest rates to calm the housing market. Future entry to the Euro could help with overall lower European interest rates being more suited to the needs of Scotland, the North East and North West than the currently nationally determined rate.

KEY WORDS

Economic activity rate of women workers	EU enlargement
Knowledge-based economy	Employment rate
Globalization	'Natural' rate of unemployment
De-industrialization	Demographic time bomb
	North/South divide

Useful websites
Other similar sites are available for different regions of the country
www.thisisthenortheast.co.uk

Further reading
Grant, S., and Vidler, C., Part 2 Unit 5 in *Economics in Context*, Heinemann, 2000.
Griffiths, A., and Wall, S., (eds), Chapter 15 in *Applied Economics*, 8th edn, Longman, 1999.
Maunder, P., et al, Chapters 12 and 24 in *Economics Explained*, 3rd edn, Collins, 2000.
Sloman, J., Chapter 9 in *Economics*, 4th edn, Pearson Education, 1999.
The World Guide 1999/2000

Essay topics
1. (a) Discuss what factors caused the rise in the participation rate of women in the second half of the twentieth century. [10 marks]

(b) Assess what is likely to happen to the participation rate of women in the next decade. [10 marks]

2. (a) Discuss the impact that globalization is likely to have on the demand for, and supply of, labour in the UK. [8 marks]

(b) Assess three policies a government could implement to solve a skills shortage. [12 marks]

Data response question
OCR, Q1, Specimen Paper 4387, 2000.

Changes in the British Labour Market

Extract 1

Table 1 shows the distribution of earnings as a percentage of the median pay of men and women in 1979 and in 1995. The median pay is the mid-point of the earnings distribution – in 1995, for example, the median pay for men was £304 per week and for women £222 per week. Consequently, as the table shows, 10% of men earned at least 186% of the median wage in 1995, whilst 90% of men earned at least 57% of the median wage.

Table 1 Distribution of Earnings as a Percentage of Median Pay

	Men		Women	
	1979 % of Median Pay	1995 % of Median Pay	1979 % of Median Pay	1995 % of Median Pay
top 10% earned more than	157	186	159	181
top 25% earned more than	125	137	125	140
top 50% earned more than	100	100	100	100
top 75% earned more than	80	74	82	76
top 90% earned more than	66	57	69	61

Note: The figures relate to gross weekly earnings of full-time adult employees whose pay was not affected by absence in April each year.

Source: Department of Employment, *New Earnings Survey*, 1997, Part A, HMSO

Extract 2
Wages Councils and Minimum Wages

The Trade Union Reform and Employment Rights Act in the early 1990s brought at least a temporary end to the 84 year old system of legal minimum wages. Until that date, it was the role of Wages Councils to determine them. At abolition, the 26 Wages Councils determined minimum rates of pay for 2.4 million workers, mostly non-union women working in the service sector - in shops, restaurants, hairdressers and so on – but also in some parts of manufacturing.

The Wages Councils did little to raise the relative pay of the low paid, but they may have prevented it from falling. The government's precise reason for abolishing the councils was unclear. Ministers sometimes implied that minimum wages priced unskilled workers out of jobs and led to higher unemployment. In defending abolition of the councils, however, former Employment Secretary, Gillian Shepherd, argued that they were irrelevant, since most workers covered by the Councils' Wages Orders earned more than the minimum rates of pay being set.

If the latter claim proved true, abolition would have had little effect other than to save the money spent on the Councils' administrative machinery. If the Councils did serve to price some workers out of jobs, however, reform should have led to more jobs, but with the consequence of even lower pay for some of the weakest groups in the labour market.

Source: Adapted from 'The Labour Market' by John Philpot in *Focus on Britain,* edited by Phillip Allen, John Benyon and Barry McCormick, Perennial Publications, 1994.

(a) Give two reasons which might explain the fact that the median earnings of men and women differed in 1995 (Extract 1).
[4 marks]

(b) (i) Using the data in Table 1, show how the pay gap (i.e. the gap between the highest paid and lowest paid) widened between 1979 and 1995. [3 marks]

(ii) Explain one reason why this pay gap may have widened.
[2 marks]

(c) (i) Use supply and demand analysis to explain why it could be argued 'minimum wages priced unskilled workers out of jobs' (Extract 2). [2 marks]

(ii) Explain the likely impact of the abolition of the Wages Councils on the pay gap for women. [3 marks]

(d) Discuss one policy which might be used to reduce earnings differences between men and women. [6 marks]

Conclusion

In considering the economics of labour markets, we often ignore the fact that labour markets are about people. Each downward shift in the demand curve for labour has a potentially devastating effect on people's lives and the social costs are frequently under valued. Companies receive the benefits of employing people but do not bear the full social costs of making them redundant. An unemployment rate of 4% sounds good but to the person who has lost his or her job it is 100%. Hiring and firing simply plays with people's lives.

If the control of labour markets is handed over to the forces of supply and demand and regulation reduced, the supporters of free markets would claim that greater job creation will be the result and increased prosperity will follow. The USA is used as a model for what can be achieved. However, greater income inequality, poverty and unemployment can be the outcome. Unemployment in the UK in the 1980s and 1990s seemed to be tolerated in order to control the trade unions and wage settlements. It did achieve this but at a heavy cost. It led to a serious waste of resources and produced households where for different generations there was no expectation of work. Idleness particularly amongst the young opened the way for the growth of the drug culture which we now have to spend huge resources to combat. Many older people now drop out of the workforce because they feel that they are not valued and have nothing to contribute.

Some regulation is needed to ensure that the powerless are not exploited too much but individuals also have to accept that they have a responsibility to keep in touch with the skills required in the modern labour market. A balance needs to be struck so that firms are given the freedom they need to develop their enterprise and creativity which will generate prosperity and jobs but protection is given to the workforce to ensure fair play in the workplace.

There are tensions from left and right. Many people look to the USA claiming that the UK would have more to gain by turning its back on the EU and joining the North American Free Trade Association (NAFTA). These Euro-sceptics seem to possess a highly selective view about what the UK's sovereignty means and conveniently forget the cultural and economic power the USA already exerts over us. A decision to join the Euro zone will lock the UK into a more EU-centred, interventionist approach and will have major repercussions for the labour market.

Interesting times are ahead and, armed with the information in this book, the hope is that you should be better equipped to consider the issues, question statements and participate fully in the key decisions about your own working life and about the economic prosperity of the UK. By the way, you should also do better in your exams as well.

Index

Accelerator 62
Age discrimination 33

Balance of payments 59
Basic skills 15
Birth rate 7, 104
Business cycle 16, 62

Closed shop 50
Common Agricultural Policy 57
Comparative advantage 58

Death rate 7
De-industrialization 57, 63, 115
Delayering 14
Demographic time bomb 106,
    116
Derived demand 6, 16, 22
Disability discrimination 33
Discrimination 31

Economic cycles 62
Economic rent 26
Efficiency wage 49
Elasticity 4
Employment
    disequilibrium 66
    rate 56, 115
Employment Service 44
EU enlargement 115
EU Working Time directive 14
Euro 58, 113
European Regional Development
    Fund 66
European Social Fund 66
Exit/voice theory 38

Family friend working 15
Fiscal policy 45
Flat rate benefit 45, 83
Flexible labour market 17
Free market economy 3

General Strike 36
Glass ceilings 32
Globalization 113
Government failure 51
Gross National Happiness 93

Hostages 38
Human Development Index
    (HDI) 93

Income 78–91
    distribution 78–91
    inequality 31
Incomes policies 47
Individual Learning Accounts 44
Inelastic supply 25, 26
Inflation 50
Insiders and outsiders 37
Institutional racism 32
Invisible items 61

Keynes, J. M. 63
Knowledge-based economy 113

Labour
    demand 16
    division of 24
    mobility 44
    theory of value 35
Laffer curve 46
Lorenz curve 79–80

Macro economic management 47
Marginal revenue product 23–5
Market failure 31
McPherson Report 32
Means tested benefit 45, 83
Minimum Income Guarantee
  (MIG) 105
Mobility
  geographical 22, 44
  industrial 22
  occupational 22
Monetary Policy Committee 70
Money illusion 68
Monopsonist 49
Moser report 15
Multiplier effect 59, 62

NAIRU 67
National Minimum Wage 11, 35,
  48, 49, 84, 98
Negative equity 85
Net migration 7, 56
Newly industrialized countries 97
North/South divide 116

Objectives 1, 2, and 3 66
Opportunism 38
Opportunity cost 13, 106

Pensions 103–8
  stakeholder 105
Perfect information 44
Perfectly inelastic 26
Phillips curve 67
Planned economy 3
Population
  age structure 8, 103
  ageing 10, 104
  dependent 104
  working 5, 56
Poverty 31, 92–8
  absolute 92
  relative 92–3

  trap 12
Presenteeism 14
Productivity gap 15
Profit sharing 25
Public choice theory 51

Quality of life 81, 93

Regional policy 66
Relative poverty 92
Restructuring 14

Sex discrimination 31
Share options 25
Single European Market 44, 61,
  66
Smith, Adam 24, 83
Social exclusion 13, 98
Sticky wages 6
Supply and demand 3, 4
Supply-side policies 71
Sustainable Economic Welfare
  Index 93

Taxes
  direct 45, 82
  indirect 45, 83
  progressive 45, 83
  regressive 45
  stealth 116
Trade unions 28, 35–8
Transfer earnings 26
Transfer payments 83
  trap 12

Underclass 98
Unemployment 56, 61–73
  equilibrium rate 67
  natural rate 13, 67, 115
  structural 63
  voluntary 13, 67

Wealth 78–87